BEING FRANK

BEING FRANK

God's strength in man's weakness

Frank Gamble
WITH MARY AUSTIN

Introduction by Terry Virgo
Foreword by Gilbert Kirby

WORD PUBLISHING

Word (UK) Ltd
Milton Keynes, England
WORD AUSTRALIA
Kilsyth, Victoria, Australia
WORD COMMUNICATIONS LTD
Vancouver, B.C., Canada
STRUIK CHRISTIAN BOOKS (PTY) LTD
Maitland, South Africa
ALBY COMMERCIAL ENTERPRISES PTE LTD
Balmoral Road, Singapore
CHRISTIAN MARKETING NEW ZEALAND LTD
Havelock North, New Zealand
JENSCO LTD
Hong Kong
SALVATION BOOK CENTRE
Malaysia

BEING FRANK

Published by Frontier Publishing International in association with Word Publishing, Milton Keynes, England.

ISBN 0-85009-553-0 (Australia ISBN 1-86258-200-9)

Reproduced, printed and bound in Great Britain for Word (UK) Ltd., by Clays Ltd., St Ives plc.

Frontier Publishing International is committed to the production of printed and recorded materials with the view to reaching this generation with the gospel of the kingdom. FPI is part of New Frontiers International, a team ministry led by Terry Virgo, which is involved in planting and equipping churches according to New Testament principles. New Frontiers International is also responsible for a wide range of training programmes and conferences.

92 93 94 95 / 10 9 8 7 6 5 4 3 2 1

For
Glenda,
my outstanding wife

Special thanks

I want to express my special thanks to Nonni (Iona Giagnoni) for typing the manuscript, to Mary Austin for her partnership in shaping the book and to Chris Wisdom for his help and encouragement.

Contents

Introduction

Knowing Frank Gamble personally is one of the great privileges of my life. Much of the process described in this book I have watched take place — from the early days when he began to walk with a slight stoop, to the present when his frail body is rarely seen without a wheelchair. Throughout this tough process I have never heard the faintest hint of a complaint against God or even caught a whiff of self-pity. His bright smile and constant flow of jokes bring an atmosphere of joy wherever he goes. When Frank enters a room the laughter level always rises.

In urging him to write his story we have had to bully him to allow us a peep behind the curtains at the pain and suffering that he and Glenda have to endure daily. 'You must tell us more about the difficulties,' we said. 'What difficulties?' he replied. Eventually he conceded and has given us a book which proves that God can sustain His children not only in the ordinary levels of testing that we all undergo, but also when some are called upon to endure the examination at advanced level.

In an age when personal comfort is almost regarded as a right and the gospel can sometimes be represented as a 'bless-me trip', Frank's story serves as a powerful reminder that life can be agonisingly complicated and purplexing. Easy answers are not always available. What is always available is the grace of our amazing Saviour. Frank shows us the way to overcome against extraordinary odds and draw on the truly sufficient grace of a wonderful God.

Terry Virgo, January 1992

Foreword

I first met Frank Gamble when he came to London Bible College to be interviewed as a prospective student. He seemed a likeable fellow, outgoing, keen on sport — particularly soccer — but, as we later discovered, probably not quite so keen on study! Most important of all, he was a deeply committed Christian.

We accepted him and he soon proved to be very popular among his fellow students. He had a brilliant sense of humour and was full of fun. Before long, he was representing the college on the football field, going on tour with the college choir, spending time with a host of friends and occasionally finding his way to the college library! Several of the close friendships which Frank formed at college have continued to this day.

We learnt that he was very fond of a girl in Suffolk and looked forward to meeting her. When that momentous day came, we decided that she was one of the most mature eighteen-year-olds ever! They were married shortly after Frank left college. It has proved to be an ideal match.

When Frank graduated I was honorary pastor of Roxeth Green Free Church in Harrow and the church invited him to become a full-time worker there. Our relationship was excellent. He started out by being my assistant but soon the roles were reversed and I was happy to be his. While we were together I had some of the richest experiences of my life.

Frank was always very gracious and on most Sundays, we shared in the conduct of the services. He introduced me to deeper worship and we saw the relevance of spiritual gifts for today's church. My complete lack of musical ability was covered by Frank's gift in that direction. The guitar came into its own and the congregation was encouraged to participate wholeheartedly in worship. Numbers grew and the sense of warm fellowship in the church was remarkable.

They were very happy years. Whenever I was preaching elsewhere I was delighted that the church at Roxeth was in such good hands. Sadly, there were a few people who were not too happy about certain changes that were taking place and one or two of them tried to play us off against each other. However, the bond between us was so strong that they had no hope of success.

It is remarkable that two men, so different in age and background, could work side by side for so long. There were very few times when we begged to differ. I suppose I was a little more cautious than Frank. I do remember saying, 'Cool it!' on two occasions: when he was anxious to do away with the church rules and when he wanted to scrap the membership roll and start afresh. He took my counsel very well.

For most of the time that we were together, it was not obvious that Frank was going to endure severe suffering, although from about 1977 he became aware that something was wrong with his health. His illness was eventually diagnosed as ankylosing spondylitis.

But it has been during the years of weakness and suffering that Frank's face has become increasingly radiant. In spite of the frequent visits to hospital and the confinement to a wheelchair all his waking hours, he has displayed a triumphant faith. Those who have visited him hoping to bring some comfort have received far more than they have been able to give. Whether in hospital or in his own home, Frank has let his light shine. I have never seen him depressed and he believes that God will eventually heal him.

In 1982 Frank and Glenda moved from Roxeth and planted a church in Stanmore. The disease was taking an increasing hold on him but Frank was undaunted. He preached as powerfully as ever from a wheelchair and the church grew. It has since moved several times because of the pressure on space and is now located in Wealdstone. Not surprisingly, the Gambles have gathered round them a very loving and warm-hearted people who have been quick to express their love in many practical ways and have made sure that Frank is relieved of any financial worries.

In more recent years, they have released him into a wider ministry. He now gives pastoral oversight to a number of churches in the south of England and accepts speaking invitations around the country. Glenda has the role of chauffeur and drives Frank around in a marvellous vehicle which has been expertly adapted to take the wheelchair.

Frank's story is an inspiration in itself. It witnesses to the power of God in the life of a man stricken in the prime of life with a fearful disease. That same grace is seen in a devoted wife who never complains and who copes with his weakness in the most remarkable way, while at the same time looking after their three lovely children, Naomi, Adam and Rebekah.

This is an unique story which I am delighted to see in print. As you read it, you will catch many glimpses of Frank's sense of humour and love for God. More importantly, you will see how wonderfully God can enable someone to overcome great difficulties and come out rejoicing.

Gilbert Kirby, January 1992

1
Bad News

I was waiting outside the consultant's office for what seemed like an eternity. Finally the door opened and a nurse came out. 'Mr Gamble,' she said, 'Dr White will see you now.' I walked into the small brightly lit room and was greeted by a warm smile. The doctor held up an X-ray of my spine and pointed to it. 'Can you see that blurring around your vertebrae?' she said gently. 'That's caused by an arthritic condition called Ankylosing Spondylitis. It's an incurable disease which will attack every joint of your body.'

Incurable. The word was locked in my mind as she spoke. I couldn't believe what I was hearing.

She continued, 'In time, your back will become stiff, your spine will curve over and your joints will calcify. The treatment is twofold: exercise to keep your joints moving and your spine straight for as long as possible, and drugs which will reduce inflammation in your joints.'

I left the hospital feeling utterly devastated. I

had never imagined that anything like this could happen to me. In the past I had been able to use my wits to get me out of difficulties. But not this time. Suddenly I was facing the biggest challenge of my life and I knew that I would never be the same again.

It was hard to imagine that just a few months earlier I had been on an active holiday in California with my wife Glenda and our two children, Naomi aged two and Adam just seven months. Our motto was *Have babies, will travel!* We visited some friends in San Francisco, camped in the beautiful Yosemite National Park, visited Disneyland and ate in every kind of eating place imaginable. But it was on a trip to San Diego that I first noticed a stiffness in my spine, and it was while I was water skiing in the harbour there that I became unusually breathless.

When we returned to England I went to my doctor. He gave me an appointment to have some X-rays taken, and on the form he wrote *a.s.?* We had some friends called Dan and Annette staying with us at the time. Knowing that Annette was a qualified nurse I asked her what *a.s.?* meant. 'It means Ankylosing Spondylitis,' she replied. 'It's not a terminal disease but if you've got it, it will bend you over and your spine will set.'

Being an eternal optimist I didn't really take it all on board. It seemed so unlikely. I was 26 years old and had never had a serious illness or been in hospital in my life. I had never even had a blood test. Besides, I regularly played football and other sports. The X-rays would undoubtedly show that I was fully fit. The stiffness in my spine was no more than a minor and temporary setback. But I was wrong. Not only did I have the disease, I had it in its severest form. Trust me never to do anything by halves!

From the moment I heard that I had the illness I did all I could think of to minimise its effects on my life. When I discovered that the drugs would have certain side effects, I decided not to take them. But I worked hard at the exercises. There were ten of these and every day they had to be done ten times each. I also exercised in a warm pool under the supervision of physiotherapists. It was called hydrotherapy and I did it faithfully for the next six years. When I noticed that a slight curve was developing in my spine, I went to an osteopath who tried to manipulate it. After several sessions he told me that he could not help me any more and that only a miracle could unlock the vertebrae because they had already begun to calcify. I took vitamin C tablets and capsules of cod-liver oil. I lay on my back and lifted weights to try and straighten my spine. I went swimming nearly every day.

But all my attempts were futile. The disease was steadily imprisoning me and I was helpless against it. In the end I was forced to accept the diagnosis: I had a progressive disease for which there was no medical cure and which would one day confine me to a wheelchair.

2
Early Years

As a child I was always full of life and getting into all kinds of mischief — ably assisted by my older brother, John, and younger brothers, David and Mark. Angela, my older sister, tended not to get too involved in our pranks.

We were brought up well. Our parents were Christians and we attended Sunday School and were taught to pray every day. From early years I had an acute awareness of God and quickly built up a knowledge of the Bible.

After Mark was born, my mother became very ill. We were living in East London at the time and the pastor of the church there prayed that God would heal her so that she could bring up her family. Miraculously, she recovered and it was only after we had all grown up, some nineteen years later, that God took her home.

I was so grateful to Him for giving her back to us. He proved to me then that He can and does heal.

My mother was an extrovert and was always full of life. She was small but very attractive, had beautiful curly hair and always looked smart. My father, a civil engineer, was more of an introvert and was much quieter. He was good-looking, intelligent and a born winner. I respected him. His firm discipline produced character and security in me. He was also very loving — especially after he had corrected me. I remember lying in bed and feeling a deep sense of comfort and reassurance as he stroked my forehead before I fell asleep. Mum and Dad had their disagreements but on the whole they got on really well and they loved each other.

But they struggled to bring up five children on very little money. My mother was physically quite frail so my father would come in from work and shoulder some of the responsibilities. He took charge of the domestic chores, did the washing and the shopping and cooked the Sunday dinner every week.

In the early years we moved home several times to keep pace with my father's work. When I was about two years old we went from London to St Ives in Huntingdon and from there to Mildenhall, Suffolk where we joined a Baptist church. From Mildenhall we moved four miles to the village of West Row. We lived in a cottage opposite the little Anglican church until I was seven and then we moved into a council house.

It was around that time that I started to enter for the local Scripture exams. This involved learning passages from the Bible and studying the parables and teachings of Jesus. I enjoyed reading the Bible and I always did well in the exams. Little did I realise then that one day I would be going to Bible college.

My father supported Aston Villa football club and wanted his sons to follow his example, so when they won we had fish and chips and when they lost, we didn't! Needless to say, we quickly learnt to look for the Aston Villa result and always hoped that the team would win.

My brothers and I were quite a handful. We frequently watched exciting programmes such as *The Lone Ranger* and *Robin Hood*. Immediately the programmes were over, out came the capes, the guns and the bow and arrows. We often dressed up in our cowboy suits, held shoot-outs and captured the villains. As Mark was the youngest he was usually chosen to be the baddy. The goodies always won and the baddy was generally tied up, put in prison or shot.

One day, much to Mark's relief, a little boy who was visiting his Auntie came to play cowboys with us. By unanimous vote he was nominated the baddy. After chasing him around the garden for most of the afternoon, we eventually handcuffed him, tied up his legs, gagged him and locked him in the garden shed. At this convenient moment, Mum called us all in for tea.

A long time later Auntie came looking for her little nephew. My mother had assumed that he had returned home when she called us in. We all looked at each other with horror. We had totally forgotten him. When we opened the shed we found a rather distressed little cowboy who, even though he was staying for a whole week, never came round to play with us again!

On another occasion we decided to make a burglar alarm. We got some old tins out of the dustbin, filled them with dry ash and tied them to the washing line which we propped up with a wooden pole. We then tied a piece of string to the bottom of the pole and pulled it across the path a few inches from the ground. If any burglar walked round the back of our house during the night, he would trigger our alarm and we would pounce. Early the following morning Mum called us all downstairs with a very cross voice. Her hair was covered with ash and she looked battered and bruised. The burglar alarm had worked very effectively when she went to use the outside toilet!

Since John was quite a bit older than the rest of us he had left home. Angela kept well out of the way, although she did referee some of our permitted boxing sessions. Mum let us put on boxing gloves so that we could have a really good punch-up. Whenever I fought Dave I tried to wallop him hard on the nose because he was prone to nosebleeds and blood brought some realism to the proceedings! It was all in good fun and we always hit Mark gently because he was the youngest and to hurt him would incur Mum's wrath.

Two very funny childhood incidents stick in my mind. My father used to cut our hair in order to save money. On the whole he did a reasonable job, but on one occasion he cut half my hair and then nicked my ear with the scissors. The sight of blood streaming down my face unnerved him so much that he decided to lick a cigarette paper, put it over the wound and leave the other side uncut. 'That will do, Frank,' he said. 'We'll leave it at that.' For the next few days I walked around half shorn. I must have looked quite a sight.

The other incident took place one morning when I was getting ready to go to school. Mum had washed my only pair of trousers and could not find anything else for me to wear except a pair of bright green knee-length jeans that belonged to Angela. She put those on me, then got a pair of Dad's patterned socks and pulled them up over my knees. 'I can't go to school like this, Mum,' I said. 'Everyone will laugh at me.' 'Don't worry,' she replied. 'Just tell them that you're a German.' I went to school that morning feeling terrible. Every day previous to this I had been English, and now, suddenly, I was telling all my friends that I was in fact a German! I'm amazed that I recovered from the experience.

Mum was a great believer in mixing brandy with water and giving it to sick children and animals. I hated it, but it seemed to work on the animals. When our rabbit fell ill we thought it was at death's door. But she put some brandy in its water bottle and it revived and lived for another five years! On another occasion we found the goldfish floating upside down in its bowl looking as if it were just about to give up its gills. The water was duly dosed and the fish turned upright, swam round and round like a demented submarine and made a full recovery. Sadly we lost it shortly afterwards when Mum was trying to refresh the water. She was pouring off some of the old water into the toilet when the fish suddenly leapt out of the bowl and disappeared down the pan. We never saw it again.

It's a wonder that my brothers and I survived those years. Some of the things that happened were really quite serious. One day we were putting cardboard into the spokes of a bicycle wheel to make engine noises when Dave sliced off one of his fingers. Mum just held it together until it was stitched. Happily it survived. Mark stuck a nail right through his hand on the day that Princess Margaret married Anthony Armstrong-Jones. And I speared my big toe with the garden fork, and scarred my chin when I fell off my bike.

As a child I was acutely aware of spiritual things and knew instinctively what was right and wrong. I never swore. I avoided rude jokes or unhelpful comments and I regretted displeasing my parents or anyone else in authority. My conscience was sharpened by my increasing knowledge of the Bible. I would always tell the truth. It was almost as if someone was continually pointing me in the right direction and keeping me from doing bad things. That is not to say that I didn't do anything wrong. There were lots of times when I was in the doghouse but I know that there was within me a desire to do what was right. I had a zest for life which was not just physical.

One day a Christian nurse visited our home. 'What do you want to be when you grow up, Frank?' she asked me. 'A missionary,' I replied. I can still remember the amazed look on her face. 'That's really good, Frank,' she said.

Looking back to that moment I realise now that even as a young boy I wanted to do something for God. My parents' faith clearly influenced my thinking, in particular my father's zeal for God. When it came to spiritual things, Dad was a constant source of encouragement. He taught me a lot about God and about what it meant to be a Christian. I saw him reading the Bible, listened to him preaching and heard him sharing his faith with others. He inspired me.

When I was ten we moved to Isleham. It was a quiet place in the fens of East Anglia — a wonderful place to grow up. My parents bought the house. It was a bungalow right on the edge of the village and it had a huge garden. They named it Aston Villa!

3
Strong Mints and Sermons

It didn't take long for us to build friendships and settle into our new schools. Tony Carpenter became my best friend and most days we would go out together to play. We had a tree hut and enjoyed climbing in the branches, scrumping and getting into all kinds of mischief. I got on well with my brothers too. We had occasional arguments and differences but whenever outside threats came we closed ranks and stuck together.

We soon learnt that a bigger garden meant more gardening. We also discovered that the more work we put into it, the more benefit we got from it. Dad bought a rotivator and we planted lots of vegetables. He used to get us to help him rake over the soil and put in the seed potatoes. We also grew a large number of flowers which were cut and boxed up for sale at market. We sowed a large lawn and planted fruit trees and bushes, built a pond and enjoyed fruit from a large strawberry patch. There was also a disused pigsty which later came back into use when Dad bought two piglets and gave me the responsibility of looking after them. Before that time, however, the pigsty was the scene of one major battle.

Dave, Mark and I had been watching an army programme on the television. When it was over we put on our green plastic helmets and ran off to the pigsty to play war games. The earth had recently been turned over and there were plenty of dry clods to throw around. When they hit the corrugated roof of the pigsty they exploded like bombs and we thought this was wonderful. Anyway, we decided that one of us would get into the pigsty and the other two would bomb him. Mark, who was then about seven, was nominated and for the next half an hour Dave and I discharged all our ammunition at him. Towards the end we could hear him shouting, 'Stop it! I can't take any more.' But we ignored his pleas and relentlessly kept up our attack. 'He's cracking,' we thought. So we continued smashing the clods of dirt at him until we heard this sort of growling noise and saw Mark's head appear over the pigsty. His face was red and he looked completely wild. We had pushed him too far. He jumped out screaming, 'I'll kill you!' We just ran for it. He picked up a hammer and hurled it at us, but fortunately we were out of range. He then found an airgun, loaded it and shot at us. The pellet whizzed over our heads as we got close to the house and I heard it go *zing* against Mum's car. We thought he was crazy. I hid in the toilet because there was a lock on the door and Dave dived into the bathroom. We stayed hidden until Mark had calmed down. I will never forget it.

Dad spent a lot of his spare time with us. He bought a canoe and regularly took us for trips up the river. We went fishing and played football, cricket and other games. My mother rarely came with us. For one thing she didn't always feel well and I think she appreciated the peace and quiet when we had all gone out. Her main enjoyment was watching old films on the TV and eating chocolates.

We were all encouraged to learn the piano. Angela and I took it further than the others. When Dad went out preaching we would also sing together as a family. My mother played the guitar and my father the piano accordion. There were many nights when I fell asleep to its strangely comforting sound.

Dad took us to Pound Lane Baptist Church where we quickly got involved in all kinds of activities. One week, my Sunday School teacher encouraged us to find a Bible verse on a building somewhere in the village. We went out to look for it and eventually found it written in big letters at the very top of the Anglican Church tower. The verse read, 'Unless the Lord builds the house they labour in vain who build it.' While I was at

Isleham I often looked up at these words and wondered why God wanted to build His house. Only later did I discover that the church wasn't a building but a people.

Our days at Pound Lane were happy. The Sunday School anniversaries were considered to be important events in the church calendar and Mrs Murphy thoroughly prepared us children for them. Her husband sat in the same pew each week — alongside the Colonel.

Colonel Thompson was a striking man. He was quite tall and had white hair and a grey moustache. He was also very strong and always full of fun. When I got to know Mr Murphy and the Colonel I used to sit on the balcony with them and listen to the sermons. Many of the other children left after the first part of the service but although I was only ten years old I wanted to stay for the whole time.

As the sermon began the Colonel would always put his hand in his pocket and pass me an extra strong mint — that kept me quiet for the whole time. After the service he would load us into his VW caravanette and drive us back to his home which was just a few hundred yards away from ours. His wife had a very bad leg and I can still picture him lifting her out of the van as if she were a feather.

The Colonel was an excellent gardener and would never let me leave without something to take home. 'Come with me, my boy,' he would say. 'Let's see what we've got.' Then he would fill up a bag with fruit. 'Wrap those pears up in newspaper, and put them in a drawer so they'll ripen,' he would tell me. He had plums and greengages too, and would always give me a bunch of flowers for my Mum. But best of all, he had the biggest strawberries you ever saw! He would take me around the back of his bungalow to rows of glass frames and pick out the biggest strawberry he could find. 'How about that, my boy?' he would ask cheerily. I needed no encouragement.

Some Sundays I would stay to lunch with the Thompsons. Because he had served in India his bungalow was filled with a host of unusual things. I remember vividly a tiger skin rug, Indian furniture and ornaments, bamboo screening around the walls, beautiful carpets on the floor and all kinds of other pictures and artefacts. It was the Colonel who taught me to play chess. I can still remember the day I beat him for the first time. 'Well done, my boy, well done!' he cried.

The Colonel was always there as I grew up. He never seemed to age or change. On the day when I half-heartedly ran away from home, it was to him that I turned. He didn't realise that he had a runaway on his hands and let me do my homework in his attic room. When my mother phoned to say that she was worried sick about me, he let me stay until I was ready to go home. Then he loaded my bag with pears and sent me on my way with a cheery smile and a firm friendly slap on the back.

My mother was so relieved to see that I was all right that she didn't scold me. Instead she reassured me of her love. I needed that reassurance. On the whole we got on really well but there were times when I seemed to clash with her because I was the most like her in temperament.

Although my mother relished contact with the upper classes, she was no snob and was always quick to support the underdog. If there was a crisis, she would get involved and do what she thought was the most helpful thing. She was overwhelmingly generous, sometimes to complete strangers, and she believed in people when others had given up on them. This meant that sometimes she was hurt or used — but she never changed.

My father preached on most Sunday afternoons. He was on the Methodist circuit for lay preachers and visited many of the surrounding villages. He would often ask me to go and sing for him and I always agreed. I enjoyed being with him and I listened intently to his preaching. His sermons were always packed with vivid illustrations and humour.

But it puzzled me why I often found myself fighting back tears as we sang hymns or as Dad talked about the cross and God's love for us. As I listened I sensed that my heart was melting and reaching out to God. I became aware of my shortcomings and felt deeply unworthy. At such times God seemed to come very close and draw me towards Him. I wondered what was going on but He had everything in hand.

4
My Biggest Decision

Some time after I heard that I had ankylosing spondylitis I returned to my consultant. She told me that at the moment I was conceived I was destined to get the disease. That revelation staggered me. Before I was even born the illness was hanging over me like the Sword of Damocles. It was inevitable and inescapable.

But there was something more incredible than this and I discovered it when I was eleven years old. It concerned a decision that had been made about my destiny not just before I was born, but before I was even conceived. That decision would affect me far more than my disability ever could. It was a deliberate decision, a decision made in secret by someone that I didn't know until 7 January 1963, the most important day of my life.

That week there was a mission at the Methodist Church in a nearby village. My father was quite excited about going to the meetings and invited me to brave the snow and join him. We had a strong sense of expectation as we drove through the fens and I can still picture the little chapel as we parked outside. The lights were blazing in the large Victorian windows and the snow glistened and crunched under our feet as we walked up the path to the door.

The place was packed and seemed to be buzzing with excitement. Many of the people had travelled from the surrounding villages and there were several familiar faces. As we started singing the first hymn there was a fervour and enthusiasm which made my spine tingle. I can't remember everything that we sang, but the one hymn which stands out in my memory and which became the theme song for the mission was *Christ Receiveth Sinful Men*. It had a great tune and a rousing chorus which went:

Sing it o'er and o'er again
Christ receiveth sinful men
Sound the messages clear and plain
Christ receiveth sinful men.

It's hard to explain what effect that old hymn had on my young heart. I grew to love it but it challenged me. It seemed to be saying something that I needed to hear, but I couldn't explain what that thing was.

Tom Butler, the visiting evangelist, was a man with great presence and charisma. He had long silver hair that touched his shoulders. I associated his looks with the mental pictures I had of the famous cowboy, Wild Bill Hickok. There was a warmth and genuineness about him and his face seemed to radiate as he spoke boldly and passionately about God's Son dying on the cross to take away our sins. I understood everything. The message was clear and vivid, interesting and gripping. And I recognised in him the same zeal and compassion that I had seen in my father.

After he had finished, I watched with fascination as people flocked to the front of the chapel in response to the call for repentance of sin and faith in the Lord Jesus Christ. Tom was clearly overcome with joy and prayed lovingly for them before he closed the meeting.

It was my eleventh birthday on 6 January 1963 and the mission was due to finish the following evening. Dad took me along for that last night and this time Angela joined us. As we arrived we could hear everyone singing *Christ Receiveth Sinful Men*. The chapel was fuller than ever and it seemed to shake with the volume of voices.

Tom Butler preached fervently again, but this time I began to feel awkward inside. Up to this time, I had thought of myself as basically good. After all, I didn't swear, I went to church a lot and I even stayed to hear the sermon. But as

Tom spoke all the good things I did seemed irrelevant and all the bad things I did seemed to surface in my heart. By the end of the message I knew that I was not a Christian. I felt convicted and condemned. For the first time in my life I acknowledged that I was a sinner.

The final hymn was *Just As I Am*. I drank in every word of it and watched as people streamed to the front. When there was only one verse to go I suddenly put down my hymn book and pushed my way along the pew past the young people with whom I had been sitting. I reached the aisle and walked along the deep blue carpet to the front. Instinctively I knelt down and asked God to forgive my sin and change my life. When everyone had finished singing, Tom led us in a simple prayer of commitment to the Lord Jesus Christ. At this point I opened my eyes and turned to the person next to me — it was Angela! My father suddenly appeared and hugged and kissed us both. He was clearly delighted and introduced us to Tom Butler, who lovingly encouraged us and expressed his own joy and thankfulness to God for our decision to become Christians.

So I was born on 6 January 1952 and born again on 7 January 1963. I thought that I had chosen God at the mission. Later I discovered that He had chosen me. I learnt the staggering truth that I had been predestined to be His child before the world was even created (Eph. 1:4,5). That night marked the biggest decision of my life. I didn't know what the future held, but I was sure that I was now safely in God's hands and that He had a unique purpose for me.

When Dad, Angela and I arrived home, we told Mum what had happened. She was naturally delighted and Dad was quick to warn us that we would now be a prime target for the devil's attacks. 'You're in a battle now, Frankie,' he said to me. 'So watch out and let God give you victory over the enemy.' I understood what he was saying and I knew that I would face times of testing and the fiery darts of the evil one. Little did I realise then how fiery those darts would one day be.

The news about my conversion was met with great joy at Pound Lane. In the following months I went out with the pastor, Eric Woodroffe, and shared my testimony. He encouraged me to preach too — even at the tender age of eleven. I praise God for his influence on my early days as a Christian.

I continued to accompany my father on his preaching trips and used to give my testimony or sing solos at the meetings. One Sunday afternoon we went to a little Methodist chapel in Kirtling which is in the wilds of Suffolk. When we arrived we were met by the organist, a Mrs Crick. 'We're not going to have many here this afternoon, Mr

Gamble,' she said. And she was right. Absolutely no one turned up — but we still went ahead with the meeting. Dad had picked five hymns and we were singing the first of those when I noticed that the large vase of flowers on the organ looked rather unstable. When we got to the third hymn I began wondering if Mrs Crick was going to notice that the vase was moving rapidly towards the back of the organ, but she seemed quite oblivious of it and just continued playing. Then during the fourth hymn the inevitable happened. The vase trembled and disappeared. There was a terrific squeal and Dad and I creased up laughing. I doubt if the organ was ever the same again.

At school, my nickname was Moses. The other boys knew that I was a Christian and I had to put up with a constant flow of light-hearted mockery and abuse from them. I gained acceptance because I could take the gibes without reacting badly and also because of my ability on the football field.

When the physics teacher, John Adkins, started a Christian Union I decided to give it my support, even though most of the boys wouldn't touch it with a barge pole. Only about half a dozen regularly attended. I went because I wanted to stand out for God. Jesus had gone through a lot for me and as a Christian I expected to be laughed at and persecuted. I decided that it was more important to be faithful to God than to court popularity from those around me.

By this time I had a racing bike which my father had bought me and had taken on an evening paper round for one of the village shops. As I cycled round the village, I used to pass a house which was rented by an American serviceman, Gene Williams and his wife, Shirley. They were Christians and I often stopped by for a cup of tea and some macaroni cheese.

Unlike some American servicemen they were not very well off materially, but they were rich in love and hospitality. When I first visited them I was amazed to discover that Shirley brewed the tea in a saucepan, so I saved up some money from my paper round and bought them a china teapot as a present. They were thrilled with it, but you can imagine my surprise when I next visited them to find that Shirley was still making the tea in the saucepan. I walked into the lounge and there in pride of place on the coffee table was the teapot full of daffodils! They obviously thought that it was a vase. I said nothing and simply drank the well-stewed tea.

At school I noticed a change in John Adkins. He was usually rather a serious teacher and you got the impression that his Christian life was one big struggle. Then suddenly he seemed to have a new radiance and cheerfulness about him. One day he called me over after a physics lesson. 'God has met me in a new way,' he said. 'I've been baptised in the Holy Spirit—just like the disciples were.' His face seemed to shine as he spoke. I could not deny that something remarkable had happened to him.

That night on my paper round, I told Gene and Shirley about my conversation with John Adkins. Gene immediately said, 'Let's pray that God will baptise us with His Holy Spirit too!' So we did. Outwardly nothing happened to me, but my heart felt warm and I sensed a new joy welling up inside me as I continued my paper round.

My days as a paper boy were numbered. A boy named Anthony Reed worked for the same shop as me and for some reason our boss, Mr Whiteman, decided to terminate his employment. His parents were very upset about it and because they lived opposite us, my mother got to hear what had happened.

That evening, just as I was about to set off on my round, she called me. 'You're not going,' she said. 'You must come out on strike because of Anthony.' When I didn't turn up at the shop, Mr Whiteman phoned to find out where I was and Mum explained the situation. He then came round to the house to try and make her change her mind. But when there was a principle at stake, she was unmoveable. I hid in the toilet and listened to their arguments. At last, having failed on his mission, Mr Whiteman left. Anthony never was reinstated, and neither was I.

5
Follower

I grew up in the sixties when young people were experimenting with drugs and sex, and when fashion was full of flowers and flares, beads and boots, tie-dyed T-shirts and long hair. Carnaby Street was famous for its boutiques, Twiggy dominated the model world, the Beatles' *Sergeant Pepper's Lonely Hearts Club Band* album revolutionised the music scene and everyone was talking about love and peace. I already had God's love and peace so I shunned immorality and marijuana and lived for Him.

The Beatles inspired many keen musicians to begin playing together in bands. Dave, Mark, Angela and I didn't want to be left out, so we started our own gospel group. I was fourteen. I learnt how to play the guitar, Dave was on drums, Mark was on bass and Angela sang. We called ourselves the Followers. A guy called Mick Bartlett joined us too. He was a superb lead guitarist but he had one flaw. He supported

Manchester United! We could not change our allegiance. We loved fish and chips far too much to do that!

The Followers played all kinds of music but majored on country and western. We practised hard and reached such a high standard that for the next few years we travelled around playing to hundreds of people. When Mick eventually left the group we changed our name to Syntonic and adopted a more heavy metal style.

The fact that I could play the guitar gave me more opportunities for sharing my faith. I sang gospel songs in assembly and at the Christian Union. One lunchtime the group actually played a concert at my school and this had a great impact on many of the boys. One later became a Christian at university.

In those days I was really fit and hardly had any illness at all. I enjoyed sport and if I was not playing cricket for the Isleham junior cricket team, I was kicking a football around somewhere.

Nearly three years after my conversion I became convicted that I should be baptised. A service was held by the river at Isleham Ferry just a few yards from where C. H. Spurgeon was baptised — not that this fact did much for my preaching! My baptism was on a warm sunny day in May. The members of Pound Lane and High Street Baptist were there, and so were my family and friends. A number of villagers turned up to watch too. I gave my testimony to the crowd and waded into the river. Tom Chipper, the new pastor of High Street, smiled warmly and took hold of my arm. 'Frank, on confession of your faith in the Lord Jesus Christ,' he said, 'I baptise you in the name of the Father, the Son and the Holy Spirit.' He pushed me gently back into the water, and the bright sky greeted me as I surfaced. I was reminded of Jesus' baptism in the River Jordan. On that occasion God had said, 'This is my beloved Son in whom I am well pleased.' How much I wanted to please my heavenly Father!

During the summer holidays I worked with Dad, usually as a chain boy, which meant that I held a staff so that the engineer could read levels. On one occasion I joined a team of Irish labourers on a building site. They were all rough and ready lads but very friendly. My main job was driving the dumper truck and loading up paving slabs.

The tea they made always had diesel floating on top of it, but when you were thirsty you drank it no matter what it was like. I remember seeing one of the men pouring weed killer on a path before it was covered in tarmac. He immediately took the watering can to the tap, filled it and then topped up the kettle to make some tea! I could not bring myself to drink it and waited ominously for someone to keel over or be sick. There was no adverse reaction. They must have had stomachs like iron.

After successfully completing my A levels, I did

an engineering course with my father's firm and went to Marlow in Buckinghamshire to be a junior engineer on the Marlow–Bisham bypass. After Marlow I went to Boreham, near Chelmsford, to work on the Ford Motor Company test track. From there I moved to Clare, near Newmarket, where I was the engineer in charge of a twelve-mile sewer run.

I continued playing in the group and took on the job of Sunday School superintendent at Fordham Methodist Church. It was great fun teaching young children. I learned a lot about communication and the importance of preparation. I also started to attend High Street regularly.

By this time Tom and Audrey Chipper were baptised in the Spirit. They were to have a major influence on my life. The manse at Isleham was always open. Any time you walked in, you would receive a warm welcome, some tea or coffee and some uplifting fellowship. It was like a spiritual haven.

Tom was like a spiritual father to me and also to many others. He was cheerful all the time and made you feel loved and welcomed. Besides being full of fun, he would always have something exciting to tell you about the Lord. Audrey was like a spiritual mother and was continually radiant and loving. She seemed to overflow with the Word of God and invariably shared a verse or passage of Scripture over a cup of tea.

Together Tom and Audrey were a vast channel of God's love and wisdom. The key to their effective ministry lay in the fact that they lived out what they taught. They were superb examples of humble and obedient servants whose faith and love inspired you to draw nearer to God. Whatever frame of mind you were in when you walked into the manse, you would feel thoroughly blessed when you came out.

God strengthened and sharpened me through their ministry. I drank in their spiritual wisdom and insights. I learnt how to feed spiritually from others and realised how vital it is to have pastoral care and fellowship from those who are pressing on with God. They guided me and stood with me through every major decision of my life. I am so thankful to God for their love and friendship.

It was at about this time that God spoke to me about tithing, so I faithfully and happily began giving Him a tenth of all that I earned. Later I would see Him honouring my obedience by providing for me in miraculous ways.

I found tremendous spiritual benefit from attending Filey Christian Crusade which was run each September by the Movement for World Evangelism. It was held in the Butlins camp in Filey, Yorkshire and I went thirteen times in all. In the early days it was overseen by A. Lindsay Glegg, a wonderful man who, although in his eighties, was full of vigour and zeal for God. My father would take us out of school for the week because he knew that we would be spiritually blessed, challenged and strengthened.

Filey became a meeting place for young people and many gospel groups. I can still remember Pete Meadows telling us about *Buzz* magazine, Nigel Goodwin reciting his poems and the afternoon jamming sessions where every guitarist and group got a chance to sing and play. We always loved the time and felt sad when we had to return home.

It was at Filey Christian Crusade that God clarified His call on my life. I went forward at one of the meetings to commit myself to full-time Christian work. I didn't know where I would end up, I just knew that I wanted my life to count for God no matter what the cost. My eyes filled with tears as we asked the Spirit of the living God to fall afresh on us. I sang, 'Break me, melt me, mould me, fill me' and really meant it. I didn't know then how God planned to respond to me.

During my teenage years, I went out with one or two Christian girls and naturally wanted my future wife to share my sense of call to serve God full-time. Although I didn't know it, my bride-to-be was actually living in Fordham which was only a couple of miles away. She travelled on the same school bus as me and attended the Methodist Sunday School where I was teaching. She was the girl whose pigtails I once tied to the school bus seat so that she nearly missed her stop! God eventually brought us together through a stick of celery.

6
New Encounters

I can't recall the exact moment when I met Terry and Joan Yaroslaw. They had moved into the village with their two children when Terry agreed to take over the pastorate of Fordham Congregational Church. On their invitation, I took my guitar and sang at their youth group one night. After the meeting, we talked together — it was the start of a precious and important friendship.

They were full of encouragement and opened their hearts and home to me. I started attending some of their Friday night Bible studies and made great friends with the young people who attended. Joan would end the evening by giving us a terrific fry-up — eggs, chips and plenty of tea, and Terry often entertained us with superb impressions of Mr Punch. 'That's the way to do it!' he would cry. Those Friday nights were full of learning and laughter.

As Terry and Joan established themselves in

the village, many young people were converted and the Sunday evening meeting after church began to grow. My first commitment was to High Street, but I used to attend the young people's fellowship at Fordham too. The manse at Fordham was the scene of one very memorable event which took place at Christmas time in 1970 when I was eighteen.

The young people were gathered for a social. In those days I was a bit of a pain because I used to show off in a crowd and do outrageous things to make an impression. On this particular night I could not help noticing how attractive the girl whose pigtails I had tied to the school bus was looking. She had long black hair, olive brown skin and gorgeous eyes, and she was sitting on the couch with some friends. Well, I hadn't got any mistletoe so I picked up a stick of celery, held it over her head and said, 'Give us a kiss!' To my surprise and delight she obliged! Her name was Glenda Hatley and a few days later I found myself walking round to her house to meet her Mum and Dad for the first time.

I was somewhat nervous as I walked up the side path to the smart little cottage. Just before I opened the gate I got a terrible shock — a huge brown curly monster with red eyes came rushing towards me, growling and barking furiously. That was my initial encounter with Barnaby, the Irish water spaniel. The fact that I ventured up the path at all confirmed how seriously I liked Glenda!

Her parents, Dick and Gladys, gave me a warm welcome. Their cottage was warm and pretty, with lots of old brass and antiques. When I first saw Dick he looked so young that I could not work out if he were Glenda's Dad or her brother! He introduced Gladys to me as 'Mum' and that is what she became — another Mum. They were not Christians and Glenda constantly prayed that they would be saved before she got married. After that initial meeting with her family, Glenda and I started going out together.

Lots of things were happening on the Christian scene. One weekend Tom and Audrey took a group of people to a Fountain Trust rally at Westminster Central Hall. There was a huge crowd at the meeting which was led by Michael Harper. It was there that I first encountered the gift of tongues. During the worship people started to sing in a strange language. Their voices were blending together in a glorious harmony and I found myself joining in.

This marked yet another significant spiritual step for me because it opened the door to the realm of the supernatural. I discovered that the purpose of spiritual gifts was to glorify Jesus and to edify His church. I began to find new release when I prayed in tongues in private, and great blessing as I learnt to prophesy.

I felt increasingly drawn to pastoral ministry. To become a pastor I knew I would need some theological training, so I applied to London Bible College to do a three-year diploma in theology. Glenda also felt a call to full-time Christian work, and if our future was together this would fulfil the sense of call that we both shared. I was offered a place beginning in September 1971.

I can still remember the look on my work colleague's face as he made the last journey home with me so that the firm's van could be returned. 'You're a fool,' he said. 'Fancy giving up a good job with good pay and prospects just to become a vicar.' He couldn't understand why I felt so joyful.

The education authority refused to give me a grant, but I was willing to trust God for all my needs because I knew that His purpose for my life was unfolding according to His plan. London Bible College was now about to experience its most severe test. Could it survive three years of Frank Gamble?

7
Bible College Takes a Gamble

In September 1971 one nineteen-year-old Frank Gamble arrived at London Bible College in Middlesex. The principal then was Gilbert Kirby, a very approachable and godly man as I came to see.

My three years there were very happy. The lectures were great. The academic standard was high and the teaching biblically sound. By the time I left I had a solid foundation to my faith and could recognise doctrinal error when it was around. I discovered how to cope with pastoral situations and was given many opportunities to speak publicly about Jesus. I also learnt how to trust God for my material needs. Money was always tight but God always gave me what I needed.

I made many close friends at college and spent a fair amount of time with Ian Coffey, Alan Dinnie, Steve Brady, David Docherty and Ian Densham. One of the African students called the group of us the Lovely Brothers. We used to meet regularly to pray and share fellowship in Ian's room, which was affectionately known as Joe's Cafe. I thank God for the many happy times that we shared together. We are all still in touch with one another and hold a Joe's Cafe reunion every year.

During my first year I started a band with three other students. We called ourselves Exodus. We played at one major concert and were able to share the gospel with many young people. We also went into school Christian Unions during lunch times and joined one of the male voice choir tours of Scotland.

College life would not have been complete without its pranks, and I was naturally keen to get involved in those! We had some hilarious times and they will live with me for the rest of my life.

The fire hose was in regular use — not for fire drill but for other purposes. On one occasion, some friends and I thought that a student named David Docherty had just gone into the toilet. He was a good friend so we quietly tied the door to the radiator and then shoved the fire hose under it and blasted him with water. We made a hasty getaway and went in for tea. But when we sat down there was David Docherty! We all looked at each other in horror and wondered who had been soaked. It turned out to be the house chairman who subsequently arrived and tried to explain to his fiancée why he was late. She was not amused and we fought to eat with straight faces as he explained what had happened.

I was not always directly involved in the pranks, but I often knew what was going on and kept quiet. Thus I was a semi-innocent observer to a joke that some of my fellow students played on Simon. He used to drive around in a bubble car which amused us. For those not able to remember what a bubble car looked like, let me explain that in shape it resembled an egg on three wheels. It was smaller than a Mini and the door at the front was largely made of glass. When you got inside you felt as though you were sitting in a bubble. Anyway, four of the guys found Simon's car, picked it up, marched it through the front door, up the stairs and through a window in the dining room. They left it on the roof. When Simon eventually discovered where it was, he couldn't believe his eyes.

Twenty-first birthday celebrations were always good opportunities for some fun. A number of us were just about to throw a student into the fish pond when Mrs Kirby, the principal's wife, came running out. 'Stop!' she cried. 'Stop!' We all thought that we were about to be told off, but to our amazement she continued, 'Give me a moment to get my camera!' She got a good shot of the event.

Our greatest laughs probably focused on the activities of Deirdre, who was a life-size cardboard air hostess that I acquired from the local travel agents. She became well-known throughout the college and appeared on several photos. She had the habit of turning up in various places and was greatly loved by all — the principal and his wife included.

Gilbert Kirby used to go to his study every evening after supper. One night before he arrived I propped Deirdre up behind his desk and left a note saying, 'Dear Principal, This is your new secretary, Deirdre.' Two or three of us then lay in wait to see what would happen. Now at the right angle Deirdre looked very real and it was dark in the office. We watched Mr Kirby go in and heard a sudden gasp. Then, after a moment he obviously gathered himself together and left with Deirdre under his arm.

Later on I met Mrs Kirby. 'Have you seen Gilbert?' she asked. 'Yes, Mrs Kirby,' I replied. 'I saw him carrying a young lady down the corridor towards the library. I think she's his new secretary.' Dear Connie didn't know whether I was being serious or not. She went off to find Gilbert and enjoy the joke.

One day Mrs Kirby wanted a few students to help her move some furniture and lay a carpet. A group of us turned up with Deirdre and decided to have a bit of fun. We stood her outside the front door, rang the bell and dashed round the side. Gilbert came out and warmly greeted the visitor, 'Hello, Deirdre! Come on in!' He then picked her up, took her into the house and shut the door. A few moments later we looked through the window and saw the principal and Deirdre locked in a passionate embrace! It was hilarious.

On the way back we stopped under the first floor window of a student called Mick Chapman. He was sitting at his desk chatting to his fiancée and periodically gazing outside. Realising that we could lift Deirdre up to first floor level, we got hold of her and stuck her face up at the window. There was a terrible scream and a terrific crash. We raced up to see what had happened and found Mick in a state of shock repeating, 'I saw a face at the window!' It was a very funny incident.

So all in all, Deirdre caused quite a stir and people still ask me how she is. At the end of my course I decided that I would leave her at college because I felt that she was needed there. Sadly, she didn't survive the pressures. I understand that on her last day she was given a lift in a dustcart and has not been seen since.

Glenda and I were engaged on her seventeenth birthday. I got together all the money I could and bought her a ring which I left safely at home. We had planned to go out for dinner together on the night of our engagement, but when we reached my house everyone had gone out and I had to break in to get the ring. I slipped this on Glenda's finger at a romantic moment during the meal. We fixed the wedding date for the end of June 1974, a month after my graduation.

In January 1973 my mother fell ill and died. The shock of losing her affected me physically and over the next few months my hair rapidly began to fall out from the middle. Two specialists said that it was unlikely to grow again and I assumed I would have to put up with looking like a monk!

One day, about three months before the wedding, I popped into the manse to see Terry and Joan. Just as I was leaving Terry asked me if anyone had prayed for my hair. 'No,' I replied. I had concluded that God had allowed my baldness to deal with my ego. But Terry felt that he should lay hands on my head and pray that my hair would grow back, which he did. 'Go on, hairy one,' he said as I left. I was full of faith that God would answer the prayer. He did. By the time I got married, my hair was thick and healthy.

God healed me again when I burst an ear-drum. It happened when my brothers and I were jamming together. My left ear popped and I instantly knew that I had done some damage to it, because when I held my alarm clock up to it I could not hear the ticking. I phoned my doctor and made an appointment to see him. On the way I called in on Tom and Audrey and asked them to pray for me, which they did. My hearing returned, but there was a slight hissing sound in my ear.

When the doctor examined it he said, 'You've got a perforation that has healed.' When I explained that the damage had been done that day, he would not believe me. He syringed my ear, a piece of skin came out, the hissing stopped immediately and I could hear perfectly. He checked my records and found nothing about a burst ear-drum. I left rejoicing in God's goodness while he sat looking very baffled.

I began wondering where I would be going after college. I was sure that God wanted me to be a pastor but I had no idea where. Glenda and I felt very peaceful about it. We knew that God would guide us and were trusting Him to do so.

One day I was walking along a corridor when I heard someone call my name. It was Gilbert Kirby. 'I've double-booked myself,' he explained. 'Could you preach at Roxeth Green Free Church near South Harrow?' He was actually the honorary pastor there.

When I went I had a really good time. The people were friendly and I felt very much at home. The next day I bumped into Gilbert. 'How did you feel it went?' he asked. 'It was a great day,' I replied. 'Well,' said Gilbert, 'I've had all the deacons on the phone this morning and they want you to go back again. I didn't tell you this, but they're actually looking for a full-time pastor.'

On the day before graduation I knew where I was going! When my fellow students asked me what I was doing after college I replied, 'I'm going to be the principal's assistant pastor.' But most of them would not believe me. They just laughed and said, 'That's a good one, Frank! Now where are you really going?'

God's faithfulness never ceased to amaze me. It was just five weeks to our wedding and He had provided us with everything we needed to begin our marriage and ministry together.

8
A Miracle for Gladys

Over the years Glenda's mother went through a number of physical difficulties and had several major operations. Her ears troubled her a lot and by early 1974 she was almost completely deaf. In spite of her poor health, she was always bright and happy to serve others.

In the months just before I graduated from Bible college, Gladys noticed a swelling in her neck. She had tests and scans and then went to see a consultant. He told her that she had cancer of the thyroid and that there were two large inoperable tumours in her neck. Then he spoke privately to Dick and advised him to make the most of the next few weeks because Gladys would not live more than three months at the most. Dick naturally went through a terrible time because Gladys meant more to him than anything else in the world.

For her part, Gladys was calm. In the early stages of the cancer she had opened her heart to

God and become a Christian. Glenda and I prayed a lot, as did the fellowship in Fordham Congregational Church. Terry and Joan Yaroslaw were wonderful and Dick was strengthened by Terry's constant visits. I encouraged Dick to see how God was healing my hair and pointed out that if God could heal me He could do the same for Gladys. We all knew that only a miracle could save her from certain death.

Since my own Mother had died, I saw Gladys as another Mum and loved her so much that I couldn't bear the thought of losing her. 'Lord,' I said one day when I was praying, 'you've taken one Mum — please don't take this one as well.'

Gladys was booked to start a course of radiation in an attempt to slow down the cancerous cells. The night before she was due to begin the treatment, Terry came round and prayed for God's healing once more. The next day Glenda, Dick and I accompanied Gladys to the hospital and I shared with her some words from Psalm 121 that God had impressed on my heart. 'I will lift up my eyes to the hills — where does my help come? My help comes from the LORD, the Maker of heaven and earth.' But it was a later verse in the same Psalm that I thought had even greater relevance for her. 'The LORD ... will watch over your life.' Gladys too sensed that God was speaking to her through another Psalm which said, 'The LORD has chastened me severely but

He has not given me over to death.'

When we arrived at the hospital, Dick, Glenda and I prepared ourselves for a long wait. But to our amazement, Gladys returned after only a few minutes. 'What happened?' we asked. 'I don't know,' she replied. 'The consultant was away and a junior doctor examined me and disagreed with his diagnosis.'

When the consultant returned some days later there was quite a confrontation over this incident. The junior doctor stood his ground and Gladys was asked to go for a further examination to see whose diagnosis was correct. The consultant, a leading specialist in this field, was amazed and dumbfounded to discover that his diagnosis had apparently been wrong and his colleague's correct. The two tumours had somehow moved which meant that they were now operable. He described them as two seeded dandelions and told Gladys that after the operation she would have to have twenty days of radiation treatment to kill off any cancerous seeds that might spread into her cells.

The operation went well and Gladys went through the horrific radiation treatment. Since she could not swallow food, she liquidised meals and tried to keep her strength up by drinking lots of milk. On the last day of her treatment I was sitting in her lounge with Dick and Glenda when Gladys suddenly called out from the kitchen. We thought something was wrong and ran to help her. But she didn't need help. When we arrived she was looking at the calendar on the wall. On it was a picture of two seeded dandelions and an obscure verse from Psalms which read, 'Their strength ... is ... cut off, and we fly away.' We were all amazed. God was telling us that Gladys was now free from the cancer. He had performed the miracle and made it possible for the surgeon to operate. Gladys is still totally free from cancer and is a wonderful Grandma to her three grandchildren and a super Mum to Glenda and me.

Gladys' healing had a profound effect on me. It strengthened my faith because it taught me that God can intervene even when humanly speaking there is no hope. Later, when I was seriously ill, I would look back at her experience, recall the way that God intervened and believe that He could heal me too.

Two weeks before the wedding Glenda's prayers for her parents were fully answered. Dick became a Christian. He had seen God at work: my hair had been restored, my ear healed and Gladys delivered from death. He knew that God loved him and had sent His Son to die on the cross for him. Now he repented from his sins and asked Jesus into his life. The change in him was immediate. It was glorious. For Gladys it had been this life that was at stake, but for Dick it was all eternity. When a sinner returns to God you see the greatest miracle of all.

9
Roxeth

The little chapel was packed with people. Someone signalled that the bride had arrived and I turned to see Glenda coming up the aisle on her father's arm. She looked absolutely gorgeous and her face was radiant as she came and stood at my side. We made our vows together, '... to love and to cherish, in sickness and in health, 'til death do us part'. Neither of us knew then that within a few years I would be facing a crippling, incurable disease. 'Through all the changing scenes of life,' we sang — an unusual hymn for a wedding, but somehow prophetic.

I felt tremendous as I walked out of the chapel with my new bride on my arm. The photographer snapped away and we were showered in confetti as we climbed into a vintage Rolls Royce to make our way to Isleham village hall for the reception. The following morning we flew to the Island of Jersey where we spent our honeymoon. We returned to the Roxeth manse which was to be our family home for the next seven years.

In early September 1974 I was inducted as the associate pastor of Roxeth Green Free Church. Gilbert Kirby led the service and Tom Chipper travelled down from Isleham to share in the meeting. There was a great atmosphere. I felt excited about the future and I was keen to lead the people into all that God had planned for them.

I was all too aware that about four months previously I had been a student and Gilbert, my principal. I was young and inexperienced and he was a mature and outstanding Christian leader. But from the outset, he treated me as an equal. In fact, he often used to tell people that he was my assistant! Gilbert was like a father to me and I was so grateful for his wise and loving input. The Lord taught me many important lessons through his godly life.

Quite a large number of people were baptised at Roxeth during my first year. Our baptismal services were incredible. Gilbert would preach and I would lead the worship. We just seemed to flow together and there was a growing freedom in worship and praise.

Gilbert chaired the deacons' meetings. They were happy times because there was a real unity and love among us. Before each meeting we would refer to the minutes of the previous meeting. On one occasion our scribe had written,

'The deacons spent the first twenty minutes looking into the manse toilet!'

The manse was a focal point for fellowship. Glenda and I wanted people to feel welcomed and loved so we opened our home to many people. Some just visited while others lived with us for a time. It was costly but we built memories and made some very close friendships.

While we were at Roxeth the church embarked on a building project and had to rely totally on God to provide the finances for it. We were amazed at the way He worked. Every time the builder wanted payment, the money was there. We borrowed nothing from the bank. I vividly remember the deacons' meeting when the treasurer stood up and announced that we had all the finances we needed — with a few pounds over. We were thrilled and gave glory to God for His faithfulness and love. The building was opened on time and gave the church some wonderful facilities for all kinds of activities. The miraculous provision strengthened the faith of many of us — not least of all mine.

There was a large estate on our doorstep and the church prayed for it and shared Jesus with the people there. We started a men's club and provided games like snooker and darts, but although we had some great evenings with those who came, none of them actually got saved which was a great disappointment. Eventually one or two did become Christians, but in such a vast estate, their conversions were very much a drop in the ocean.

Sunday morning meetings remained fairly traditional but there was greater freedom in the evenings when people began experiencing a new touch of the Holy Spirit and started using spiritual gifts. We were spoilt for good musicians and blended together the more traditional hymns with the newer songs. Gilbert and I jokingly referred to ourselves as the *Ancient and Modern*! Our primary focus was not on the age or newness of the songs, but on whether the Holy Spirit was directing the meetings. And our praise was not fuelled or governed by our feelings, but by the truth of God's Word which was expounded at every service.

I began attending meetings where people of vision like Arthur Wallis and David Watson spoke about God's purpose for His church. I discovered that worship, spiritual gifts and good relationships were vital elements in restoring the church to its original beauty.

Glenda's parents visited us regularly. They would arrive on Saturday afternoons loaded up with meat, vegetables and various other supplies. Dick would often tidy up the garden and do practical jobs around the house, while Gladys made us curtains and clothes and cooked supper on Saturday night and lunch on Sunday. Just having them around was a tremendous blessing. They couldn't have been better in-laws to me.

From the earliest days of our marriage we would often drive up to Fordham for a short break. If we left after the Sunday evening service we could be there for supper and spend Monday, our day off, in the country. One of the things I enjoyed most was going fishing with Dick. He taught me how to tie knots in fishing lines and how to ledger. He regularly took me to a huge lake that we called the Big Pit.

On one occasion we got up early, loaded up the equipment and set off for a morning's fishing. We parked the car, lugged our gear across a field to the lake and started getting ready to fish. At that moment, Dick suddenly clutched his back. 'Oh no,' he said, 'my back's gone. I won't be able to fish now.' 'Well, let me pray for you,' I replied. I laid my hands on his back and prayed. When I had finished he looked at me and said, 'The pain's totally gone.' We sat there and praised God for His immediate answer to my request.

That morning we had one of the best times ever. We landed fish after fish — most of which weighed at least a pound. Suddenly Dick shouted, 'I've got a monster on here.' I left my rod, grabbed the landing net and went to join him in the battle. Dick fought the fish for what seemed like an eternity. He needed all his strength to beat it — his rod was bent right over and his line whistled under the strain. There was nothing better to test a healed back.

Eventually the fish came to the surface. It was a tench — one of the best fighting fish that you can catch. I slipped the landing net under it and the battle was won. 'What a fish!' exclaimed Dick, who by then was totally worn out. It weighed over three pounds. We went home rejoicing that our trip had been so successful. God had blessed us with a wonderful catch, but more importantly, He had shown us a miracle of healing in response to my prayer of faith. As I returned I could not help feeling a sense of awe and wonder for everything that He had done. We shouldn't be surprised at these things. After all, God has done miracles on the edges of lakes before.

Our daughter Naomi was born in June 1975 and on Valentine's Day two years later we had a son, Adam. I was at the prime of life, happily married with two small children when, in October 1977, I heard the devastating news that I had a crippling disease.

Early disbelief eventually gave way to reality. I knew that God had already done a great deal in my life and that He was still working out His purposes for me. The circumstances were hard, but I looked at them in the light of God's goodness. I trusted that whatever happened I was secure in His love and that He would help me.

I carried on preaching and pastoring but the illness began to assert its grip on my body. Many times I would hold onto the pulpit for support and preach through the stabbing and unrelenting pain in my spine. At that time, the rest of my joints were not affected, but gradually my hips and shoulders began to hurt as well.

Then, for the first time in my life, I started experiencing hostility and mocking because of my disability. One day I went swimming and in the changing room I overheard a boy talking to his father about me. 'Look at that man's funny back!' he said. Then they both laughed at me. I didn't let them know that I had heard their conversation but I was deeply hurt.

On another occasion I was walking down the road after a heavy snowfall. Two teenage boys were walking towards me on the opposite side and I was stunned when they began making snowballs and pelting me with them. 'You're a freak!' they shouted. 'Push off, freak!' I couldn't defend myself against them so I just kept walking and concentrated on keeping my balance. The inner pain seemed almost worse than the physical agony that I was suffering.

In 1980 I was given the opportunity to go on a trip to Israel. An older couple in the church had booked to travel together, but since the wife was not feeling well enough, I took her place. Some friends offered to pay for Glenda to go too but because our third child, Rebekah, had been born only a few months earlier, she felt that she should stay behind and look after the children. I had an unforgettable time in Jerusalem and Galilee. That holiday would have been impossible later. God knew that and I was so grateful to Him for the provision.

God often provided for us in wonderful ways. On one occasion we were due to go for a week's holiday in a bungalow in Verwood, but all the money we had in the world was fifty pence, and we didn't think that was enough for petrol and food! We decided to say nothing about our needs and on the day of our departure simply started packing to go. As we were getting ready, an envelope came through the letterbox. Inside it was a gift of seven pounds. Half an hour later another envelope arrived. This contained ten pounds. Four or five more envelopes fell on our mat and each contained a sum of money. We eventually set off with eighty pounds in cash — and the original fifty pence.

10
Changes

During my last few years at Roxeth God had been sharpening my vision of the church. I found a growing burden in my heart for God's people to be all that He had intended them to be. I believed that He had begun to restore His church as an expert restores a priceless painting: removing the grime of tradition and bringing the church back to her original beauty. Apostles and prophets were being put back alongside evangelists and pastor/teachers in order to equip God's people to serve Him effectively and to bring them to maturity and unity of faith.

Glenda and I had attended the Dales Bible Week for a number of years. It was there, among other places, that we received excellent teaching about the church. It was also at Dales that I met Terry Virgo for the first time. My heart was joined to his in a remarkable way. Actually, it was one of Terry's messages there that confirmed to me that God wanted to heal me.

I also attended a number of conferences and leaders' days in different locations. One place I visited was Bedmond in Hertfordshire. Alan Vincent was leading a growing work there and he had a powerful teaching ministry. He was full of God's Word and the Holy Spirit, and his outstanding wife, Eileen, was a mighty woman of faith. The first time I met Alan, he put his arms around me and gave me a great big hug. I felt the love of Jesus flowing from this gentle giant of a man and over the following months we formed a close friendship and met regularly with the other leaders at Bedmond. Alan's vision, zeal and love for the Lord sharpened me spiritually more than ever before. I found in my heart a fresh hunger for God and a willingness to serve Him, no matter what the cost might be.

During my last few months at Roxeth I met regularly with Alan and the other leaders of the churches that he was overseeing at the time. They often prayed for me and encouraged me to seek God for healing. I didn't realise it then, but by putting me among these men God was preparing me for the next phase of my ministry.

Glenda and I never thought that we would ever leave Roxeth but in 1982 we began to feel that the time had come for us to move on.

I shared our thoughts with Alan and Terry. They weighed the matter, sensed that it was

God's will and assured us of their love and support as we stepped out in faith. It was the hardest decision of our lives, but we thoroughly tested what we believed God was saying to us, and then shared with the church that we sensed that He was calling us to pioneer a new work elsewhere. What made things hard was the fact that the 'elsewhere' was actually only a few miles away. It would naturally have been a lot easier if we had moved some distance from the area.

The whole family had to bear the cost of following God's will for our lives. The children had to wrench themselves away from their friends and find new ones in another school. We needed a new home and had no obvious means of support. But as we stepped out in faith and obedience we experienced yet another miracle of provision.

We found the ideal house in Harrow. The problem was, we couldn't afford it—so we prayed continually about it and God stepped in. Alan and the brothers at Garston decided to guarantee me a salary after we left Roxeth, so this meant that we could get a mortgage. We then prayed about the money for a deposit and in one week received three unexpected gifts that totalled exactly the amount that we required. There was a large shortfall between the mortgage and the price of the house. We decided not to make this public but rather prayed that God would confirm the step that we were taking by providing the finances that we needed.

A number of friends gave us gifts, but on the day before completion we still had only a tenth of what we required. I was away at a conference for that weekend. Just as I was leaving, someone pushed a brown envelope into my pocket. 'I hear you're moving,' he said. 'I want to stand with you.' The envelope contained a large cheque. When I got home in the afternoon, the treasurer at Garston phoned to tell us that a significant number of 'love gifts' had been handed in for us that morning.

In the evening I preached at Roxeth on the widow's cruse of oil which never ran out during a time of famine. I didn't speak on this because I was in a similar situation to the widow. Rather, I had been working through the story of Elijah and just happened to come to this particular passage on that particular day.

More gifts flowed in. We were overwhelmed and the children were thrilled because they too had been praying for God to meet our need. Seeing the way that God was answering us, one good friend remarked, 'It's just like a miracle that you read about in books.' The following day we walked into the solicitor's office with the full amount and the house was ours. God had opened the windows of heaven and poured out a blessing that we could hardly contain. He is so faithful!

11
Harrow

We moved into our new home on 6 April 1982 and spent the next six months with the church at Garston. It was a welcome break for a weary pastor and his family! We spent time getting to know the people, and then Alan called together the Harrow contingent, which numbered about 30, and told them that I would be starting a new work in the Harrow area. Most of them were keen to be part of this planting and in October we hired an old school building and began meeting together.

After only two weeks, numbers had risen to between 40 and 50. When we were invited to take over the work at Stanmore Free Church, their building became our home for the next few years. When we packed that, we began hiring a school in Wealdstone.

By this time the pain in my spine had grown steadily worse. As predicted, the discs were disintegrating, the vertebrae were grinding together and I was being forced to walk with a stoop. My neck became increasingly stiff and my breathing was restricted by the loss of movement in my rib cage. On occasions I could not sit, stand or even lie down for any length of time, and I didn't know what to do with myself. Clearly I could no longer work through my exercise sheet, and the pain killers brought only temporary relief. I didn't want to be dependent on tablets anyway, so I took them only when I was desperate.

Life became one big ordeal. Dressing was painful and increasingly difficult; lifting heavy items was impossible; driving the car required more effort and concentration and I could no longer run and play with the children. My weight dropped from over ten stones to seven and a half stones and I began to experience acute frustration and severe tiredness. I started using a walking frame in the house and eventually gave up driving because I was finding it impossible to look left and right at a junction. Climbing the stairs became an ordeal. I had to go up on all fours and pull myself up using the wooden pillar at the top. Coming down was easier but I had to cling tightly onto the bannister because falling could have been fatal.

Washing was another problem. I reached the point where I could not sit either in the bath or on the shower seat. One day Glenda blew up the children's paddling pool and put it in the bathroom. We thought that if I sat on a chair in it I could use the shower and the water would be collected in the pool. But the pool collapsed half way through my shower. I almost froze and the bathroom was flooded. Water seeped into the kitchen below and turned the ceiling a nasty brown.

As the disease kept up its unrelenting attack on my body, I became acutely aware of the effect it was having on Glenda. She was coping bravely but my suffering was traumatic for her. When things went wrong I got worked up and she was the target for my frustrations. The aggression that I mustered to fight the excruciating pain all too often found its outlet in anger, complaint and criticism which only added to the weight that Glenda was already carrying.

I can vividly remember the day when I could no longer climb the stairs. We phoned some of the men in the church and they came and moved our bed to the ground floor. Then the Social Services stepped in. They installed a lift, removed the bath and built a new shower. I also took delivery of a wheelchair which gave me greater freedom to move around.

As I was going downhill physically, the church was going uphill spiritually and numerically. Through prophecy, God told a group of leaders that if we drew closer to Him we could get alongside others and disciple them. So that is exactly what I did. I sought God and spent much of my time training men. I shared whatever revelation and knowledge I had and I taught them doctrine which would give them a good foundation for their life and ministry.

One outstanding example is Mike Thompson who became an elder in the church and then moved to Kent to lead Emmanuel Church, Maidstone. While he was with me he was a real example of godliness and love. Mike O'Connor, Barry McKaine and Richard Giagnoni met with me for six years and drank in all the doctrine and Bible teaching that I could give them. They were later joined by Clive Da Silva. I loved them all like sons. Mike and Barry have moved away but Clive still attends the church and Richard is an elder.

Richard Theobald, Mike Green and Ian Ravens were among the original group that came out of the church at Garston. Through the years I spent time talking to them and teaching them. They are now not only friends but men of godly character who have also also taken on the responsibilities of eldership. I worked with Ray Partridge too. From the moment I met him I was struck by his love and faithfulness. Glenda and I had the joy of bringing him together with his wife, Jo — who is Colonel Thompson's granddaughter. At their wedding reception Jo's father handed me a 'Frank fixed it for me' badge and I in turn presented it to the bride and groom! Ray is now an elder in Harrow. In 1988 we had the joy of seeing 33 people leave to plant a new church in South Oxhey. The people there are under the leadership of Grahame Atkins and Terry McGovern — two more outstanding men who saw the new work double in size over a very short time.

As God blessed us, I became more and more convinced that the local church was His means of bringing growth and fruitfulness to his people. I wanted evangelism to be based in the local church and new converts to be added to it. I also began thinking about my own role. As quality men were emerging in our ranks, was God calling me into a new sphere of ministry for Him?

12
This is My Life

My ministry may have been at the point of expansion, but I was struggling physically. The disease was doing to me exactly what the specialist said it would — seizing up my joints and bending me over.

In more recent years the rate of deterioration has slowed down. From time to time I notice a very slight change: I can't open my jaw as much as I could; there is a bit less movement in my knees. Eventually the disease will burn itself out. Then I will be stuck with whatever damage it has done to me.

Pain is part of my life. People ask me how I cope with it, but when you've got something all the time, you think of it as normal and put up with it. One day you might come up to me and ask, 'Are you in pain now?' and I will answer, 'No'. What I mean by that is that I am not in severe pain. But if you had my usual pain load, you would probably be saying, 'I feel awful.' My pain threshold is so high that when I go to the dentist for treatment I don't bother with an injection. He could probably drill on the nerve and I would consider the discomfort very small compared with what I've experienced with my arthritis.

A lot of people look at me and think that I can stand up or stretch my legs, but I can't. I am actually the shape that I am in the wheelchair. My spine is locked and my knees are bent at right angles all the time — even when I am in bed. I can't turn or relax my head because my neck is stiff, and I find the lack of movement very tiring.

For Glenda and me, every day is a struggle. I don't rise at the crack of dawn because getting up early means spending fourteen or fifteen hours in the wheelchair. This tends to result in pressure sores because I can't move much. So I usually get up at about ten, or earlier if I'm going somewhere or if someone's calling. I have had to learn to pace myself.

We've got the lightest possible duvet on the bed because my knees are so delicate. If we go and stay anywhere we sometimes take the duvet with us because we know it's OK. In bed I lie on a sheepskin because it prevents pressure sores. I can sleep only on my back or on my right side, and it's a real effort changing from one position to the other. Whenever I move I wake up, so I'm probably conscious for at least two hours or more out of seven or eight. It's been years since I've slept through the night. My sleep is very light too. If you speak to me, I can always answer you. Sometimes I just lie there and the pain won't leave me alone. That's miserable but I've just got to accept it.

I take painkillers only on very rare occasions. That's because I don't want to live on them. If I were regularly on pills, I wouldn't know if I were in pain or not, and I want to know. Besides, drugs can lose their effectiveness if you take them too much, so if I use them sparingly they tend to work well.

It takes Glenda about half an hour to get me up in the morning — unless I have a shower. Then it's more like an hour. The time can vary according to the level of pain I'm experiencing too. My back rarely hurts because it's virtually rigid, but where I have slight movement in my joints I'm very fragile. That's why I have such trouble with my knees. They tend to be vulnerable when I'm trying to transfer from my wheelchair to, say the bed or the shower, and even the slightest pressure on them can be agony.

To get me up, Glenda has to push my feet over the edge of the bed and rock me into a sitting position. It takes my body a little while to adjust to that because my muscles are all tense. She then dresses me. Putting trousers on is difficult when your legs can't bend, but the worst bit is often the socks — particularly if my knees are bad. Sometimes I'm crying out in pain and Glenda is in real distress. I tell her, 'Don't worry, darling. It'll be over in five minutes.' I simply want to push through the pain quickly because I know that I'll soon be in the chair and able to recover.

Having a shower is another terrible experience. The Social Services couldn't find me a suitable shower chair so I kept trying different ones. In the end a friend bought one for us, but we had to make a cushion for it and cover that with a plastic bin liner to make it waterproof. It was the best we could do. Glenda has to sit me on the chair and lift me up an inch into the shower. That often jars me and causes me pain.

I can wash most of my body but I can't reach my hair, my feet or under my arms. She has to do those. She has to cut my toenails too. That's another traumatic thing. I'm terrible about my toenails. I keep thinking she's going to cut my toes off! When someone holds your foot, it tickles and if you've got bad knees, the pain shoots up your leg and it's like torture. But to return to the shower, Glenda often feels boiling hot while I'm freezing because I feel the cold so quickly. On one occasion she nearly passed out which could have been disastrous for us both.

Transferring to the wheelchair is another hurdle. I've hurt my wrist pushing on the bed trying to get into that. Once I sprained it quite badly and had to nurse it for a while. It's annoying having to cope with additional aches which are not directly related to the disease at all.

Only when I get downstairs can I begin to relax. I sometimes go out and see people, but not as much as I used to because outings are such major things to organise. I can't just pop down the road, and if we do go out, we plan in advance when we're coming back. So I usually spend the day around the home.

In the morning I'll probably read the Bible, pray and study. I might have some visitors too. I usually arrange to see people late morning or early afternoon because it's easier for me then. Until recently I've had all sorts of evening meetings to attend.

Mealtimes can be difficult. Over the years my jaw has seized up and I can open my mouth only about a centimetre. It's always hard to eat and if the arthritis is bad, it's painful too. I tend to avoid chewy food like steak because it takes a long time to consume and everyone's waiting for me to finish my meal. But I do have a balanced diet and I sometimes supplement it with vitamins. Food steadies my metabolism. I need regular meals and hot drinks — particularly in the winter because otherwise I get very cold. When that happens it takes hours to get my body back to normal temperature. I can't fight it myself. I'm just physically weak.

Glenda can leave me alone in the house, but only for a couple of hours. That's because I'll need to go to the loo or, in winter, a hot drink and someone to turn on the lights for me. I can't use a normal toilet, even one for disabled people, so I have a commode. If we're going out for any length of time, we take it with us. I'm fine for short times on my own. I can wheel myself round downstairs, use the remote control to turn on the television or stereo, answer the phone and switch on the central heating with the broom handle. I can't make myself a drink or answer the door, but if I need help I can ring my neighbour or someone from the church.

I don't let pain affect my prayer life. It's difficult to concentrate on prayer if you're in a lot of pain, but I always try to have regular times with God. I often pray when I'm in bed, travelling or relaxing.

Pain won't stop me visiting someone or preaching either. I can remember one awful day. I was due to speak to about five hundred people at a Sunday morning meeting in Sidcup. I went to bed the night before and didn't sleep a wink because my knees were so terrible. Next day I took some painkillers and got up at 7.30. I felt sick. We loaded the car and crawled round the M25 in thick fog. I preached, and on the way back had to fight to keep awake. I can't let my body drop forward because it makes me jump when

I'm startled, and that's really painful. When we got back I had to keep going because I was preaching that evening too. After the service, people said to me, 'You're looking well, Frank.' And I thought, 'If only you knew.' God's grace helped me that day. I preached not in my own strength, but in His. He is always faithful to me.

If I'm not out late, I tend to retire at 7.30 or 8.00. Glenda will undress me, help me transfer to the bed, and rock me into it. I'll probably have a cup of tea through a straw. That's the only way I can drink tea in bed. I may then watch some TV or listen to some music, and the children might come in for a chat. Glenda and I often talk over the events of the day before we go off to sleep. I always feel very thankful to God as I rest my head on the pillow and close my eyes.

13
A Perfect Partner

It was a very touching moment. Glenda and I had finished our meal in an Indian restaurant and were just about to leave when all the staff unexpectedly lined up beside us. Their spokesman then addressed Glenda, 'Can we just say that we're very impressed by the way you care for your husband. It's very unusual to see such devotion in western society.' We had not been aware that they had been watching us. We were simply being ourselves. But even in the short time that we had been there, they had seen something wonderful in my wife's commitment to me.

A lot of people have come up to Glenda and said, 'I just want to say how much I appreciate you.' She thinks that they are just being kind — because she can't see how much she shines. But I understand exactly what they mean. No one could have coped better with the demands and difficulties that my sickness has brought. Her devotion to me has been truly remarkable; her constant care for me, her faithfulness and spiritual support, totally outstanding. She is always the same gentle, gracious and cheerful person. I could never have managed without her and I feel unworthy of her. God chose in Glenda the perfect partner for me.

We both know that we have been caught up in His purposes. In other words, Glenda doesn't think that it is just her 'bad luck' that she married me. Rather, she considers that what we are experiencing together is as much God's plan for her life as it is for mine.

I look at some marriages and think, 'They haven't got what we've got. We're much closer, much happier.' There is a rapport between us. We are often thinking the same things or I'm wondering if Glenda has done something and she will come and say she has done it without my even asking her. When you consider that we are together virtually 24 hours a day, it is wonderful that our relationship is so good. Some people think that when there is a disability, things are bound to get worse. But in our case the reverse has happened. Our marriage has actually improved and our love for one another has deepened. Why? Because God has been at work in us. His amazing grace is clearly evident in our lives.

Naturally we have had to adjust to one another.

Our temperaments are poles apart. But marriage is all about adjustment and compromise, and we are no different from anyone else in that respect. It has been particularly important for us to keep the lines of communication open all the time. That is because we do nearly everything together so if there were any bitterness between us, we would find it very difficult to keep going without talking it through.

In the early days of our marriage I was not very good at communicating. I was also rather dominant, selfish and unreasonable at times. I used to shut my ears to what I didn't want to hear and try and force my ideas onto everyone else. I was effectively saying, 'Don't get in my way. It doesn't matter what you feel like. I'm going for it, so duck!'

When I became ill I tended to be very demanding and insensitive towards Glenda. I would see something I wanted to do, but because I couldn't do it I would try to force it on her. As far as I was concerned, I would think,'That needs doing so come and do it, and do it exactly as I tell you.' I didn't consider that she might have been in the middle of something else, that she didn't have the resources available or that she could do it equally well in a different way.

I have since learnt to consider her feelings more. When she doesn't come as soon as I should like, I wait patiently for her to finish what she is doing. We talk through difficulties more than we did in the early days. I have stepped up my use of the word 'Sorry' and put things right quickly when that was necessary. We pray more together too.

As a husband I think I'm more of a strength to Glenda than I was. I used to get on with things myself, but now we tend to make major decisions together. Of course, I would love to be a 'normal husband' and take responsibility for dealing with the bank manager and so on. But as it is, she must do such things for me and I must be content to relate everything through her.

Coping with pain has been difficult for us both. If Glenda is trying to dress me and my knees are bad, I can become very aggressive. In her ears I sound angry with her, but this is not the case. I am actually trying to push through the pain. We have learnt that it is not helpful to attempt to sort out the problem when I'm in agony. So we talk about it later. I have had to watch my tongue and she has had to understand that any unhelpful comments that I might let slip are related to the excruciating pain, not to her.

Glenda has changed too. In the early days she lacked self-confidence, and I can't say that I did much to encourage her. She was almost too nice to people and they used to walk all over her. But now she is much more confident and ready to stand up for herself if she is being short-changed.

Of course, my illness has meant that she has had to throw herself into things that she might otherwise have abandoned. She learnt to drive when she was seventeen, but because she was rather nervous about it, she gave up for about ten years. Then suddenly I couldn't drive and she had to, so she did. Now she takes me all over the country.

I sit in the wheelchair behind Glenda and give directions as appropriate. Unfortunately, I have earned the reputation of being a back-seat driver, but God is working on me. The other day I was in the car rabbiting on about how she should drive when we passed a billboard which was encouraging people to wear rear seat belts. In huge letters it read, PLEASE BELT UP IN THE BACK! I was stunned into silence. 'Do you think that's a prophetic word?' I asked Glenda. 'Definitely,' she replied. We laughed and I stopped instructing for the rest of the journey.

It is good to have humour in the midst of pain because if we were serious all the time, we would be miserable. The Bible says, 'A cheerful heart is good medicine' and we often laugh at situations that we have encountered. Sometimes we have been laughing so much that I have had to tell Glenda not to encourage me because it hurts.

We appreciate the good times that we have had together, but life is hard for us all the time. Not only do I experience the physical pain, I also suffer watching Glenda endure so much for my sake. She doesn't say too much about it, but sometimes she feels overwhelmed by the situation. It is wonderful then how God steps in to encourage and strengthen her. One of those occasions was at a lead elders' and wives' weekend. But I'll let her explain what happened.

It was a few years ago. Things were really difficult. I was feeling physically unwell and just didn't know how I was going to cope. I was desperately trying to stay on top of everything because I thought that Christians shouldn't be overwhelmed and sad, but the pressure was almost too much. So before we went away on this weekend, I really wanted God to do something for me.

We had a great time, but the most precious moment came at the last meeting on the Sunday morning. It was during the worship time. I was standing saying to God, 'Please, if it's possible, could Frank be healed now? I don't think I can cope for much longer.' Then I began thinking about Jesus in the Garden of Gethsemane and how He said to His Father, 'Take this cup from me; yet not my will, but yours be done.' So I continued, 'But if it's not your will, then I'll do whatever you want.'

Just at that moment one of the leaders'

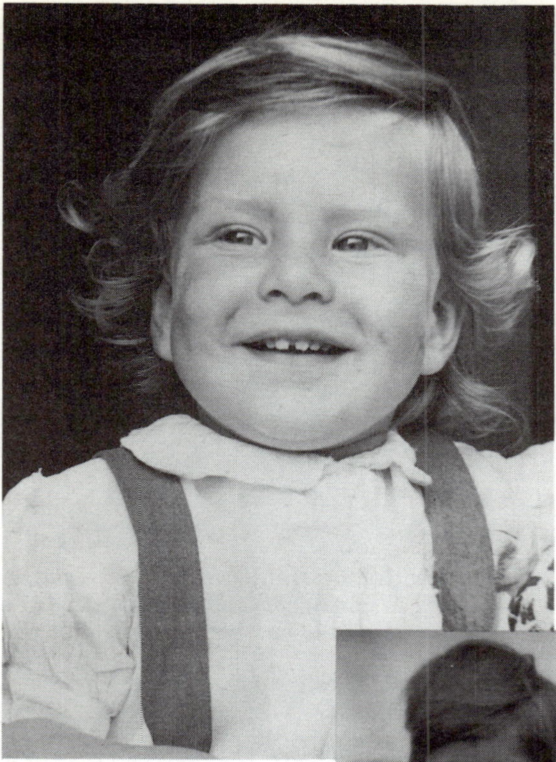

Frank (18 months).

Early Years (7).

Frank *(back row)* with his parents, Alfred and Yvonne, brothers Mark *(left)*, David *(right)* and Hazel Kemp (who asked him what he wanted to be when he grew up).

Frank (10).

"Aston Villa."

At Filey.

At Filey *left to right:* Angela, Dick Bye, Mark, David, Mick, Frank, Frank's parents.

Baptised at Isleham Ferry (14). Accompanied by Eric Woodroffe with Tom Chipper in the background.

The Followers (early group).
Left to right: Catherine Sumpton, Angela, Frank, Dave, Mick Bartlett, Mark.

School football team.

The Followers (after Mick and Catherine had left).
Left to right: Frank (17), Angela, Dave, Mark.

Frank (20) at Bible College.

Alan Dinnie, Ian Coffey, Deirdre and Frank.

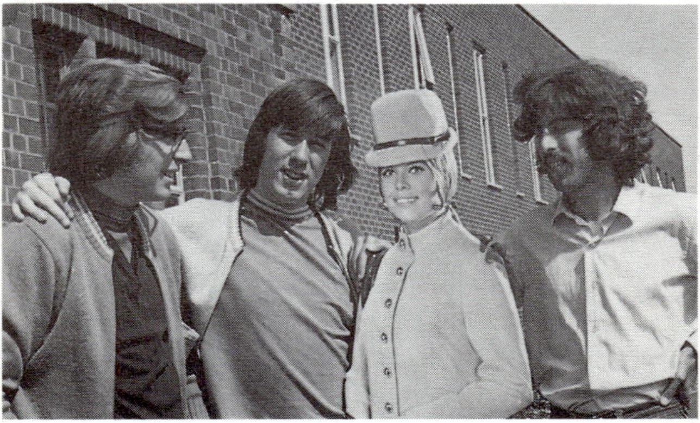

Working as a gardener at Bible College.

Special day in 1974 Frank (22), Glenda (18).

Frank inducted as associate pastor of Roxeth Green Free Church (11/9/74). *Left to right:* Tom Chipper, Glenda, Frank, Gilbert Kirby, John Balchin.

Happy family, Frank (27), Naomi, Adam, Glenda and baby Rebekah.

Father and son.

Frank's Dad, Alfred.

Glenda's parents, Dick and Gladys.

Frank (31) beginning to stoop.

Sharing the ministry with Gilbert at Roxeth.

Camping at Downs Bible Week (not yet permanently in a wheelchair).

Frank and Glenda at a Caribbean fancy dress party.

As the Lone Ranger at his 39th birthday party.

Speaker at Downs Bible Week.

A perfect partner.

By the Thames (1991).

Christmas (1991) *left to right:* Naomi, Rebekah, Frank, Glenda, Adam.

Speaker at Stoneleigh Bible Week (1991).

> wives came up behind me and started to prophesy. She was crying and crying as she spoke. 'It's a bitter cup that I've given you,' she said. Then she went on, 'But I understand how you feel and it's OK if you cry.' God then told me that there was going to be a glorious resurrection for my family and me. It was such a significant time and when things are hard I hold onto God's Word and believe that one day Frank will be healed.

Glenda and I live in constant dependence on God. I would give the world to change our circumstances. But they are in His hands. We have our spiritual highs, but generally we just get on with life. We don't always understand what is happening, but we know that He is with us and listens to our prayers. When things are tough, we draw on His grace and He sees us through.

It is wonderful how God has touched our marriage and helped us to adjust to all sorts of situations together. Many couples have lost the romance in their relationship; they take one another for granted. We could so easily do the same. But we work at love and overcome the physical barriers together.

Because Glenda does most things for me, I must make sure that I initiate things. I can't leap out of my wheelchair and hug her but I can call her over, put my arm around her and tell her how much she means to me. It sometimes hurts me just to do that, but I want to make the effort because I love her.

Occasionally I take her out for a meal, send her a bunch of flowers or book us into a hotel for a couple of days because I know that she needs a break. Sometimes I just want to spoil her with some expensive perfume. It's my way of saying, 'Thank you for everything you're doing for me.'

14
Reactions

I am so grateful for my children. At times I have felt deeply inadequate as a father and have worried about being an embarrassment to them. They have naturally been affected by my disability and all the resulting frustrations. But they have stuck by me in a wonderful way and have done many practical things for me in the home. The love we have for one another has become more and more precious to me. If I had to decide between being physically whole or loved, I would choose to be loved.

My disability has taught the children to be sensitive to others who have similar difficulties. Becky, our youngest, thinks of me as an ordinary Dad and refuses to join those who make jokes about handicapped people. Naomi, our eldest, was recently saying how annoyed she gets when able-bodied individuals park their cars in the bays which have been provided for the disabled.

Adam too understands something about pain and immobility. When he broke his leg, he was in plaster for about six weeks and nearly went crazy with frustration because he couldn't do anything he wanted.

Although we can't do many activities together, we have gone out for picnics, barbecues and the occasional concert. Since Glenda and I are often away at weekends, we periodically have special family meals together. The children try to keep every Monday night free because that is when we have our family time. I initiate and lead this. Sometimes we have a treat — a video or some nice food. It varies. We have to be flexible. One of them might want to go out somewhere, so on that occasion, we have just a short prayer time together. Otherwise, we read the Bible, talk and pray for each other at greater length.

Holidays are difficult to arrange because it is hard to find somewhere that is suitable for all of us. I need comfort, good facilities and warmth which increases the price a bit. We have been to Centre Parks which cater specially for the disabled. The villas there are all kitted out and I can get everywhere. The children enjoy it there too. But Felixstowe is our usual holiday haunt. The children stay in their grandparents' caravan while Glenda and I stay in another caravan a short distance away. It works well. I feel I can relax there. We have stayed in other places but find that it can be more hassle than it's worth.

Glenys Venn, our next-door neighbour, is almost a part of our family. One day, we asked her to look after the children, and she soon became our regular babysitter. If I am preaching she will sometimes cook them Sunday lunch, and if we are away for a weekend, she will look after everything. When we return, we will often discover that the house has been cleaned from top to bottom and that all the ironing has been done. She is marvellous, and so trustworthy and conscientious too. The children call her Grandma Venn and have all really grown to love her.

But it is a mutual blessing. She enjoys the contact with our family too. She comes round most days and if she ever needs us, we are there. When Glenda's parents visit us they often bring her some steak — Dick's a butcher — and they might invite her round for Sunday lunch or supper. Sometimes Dick will play a few tunes on the piano and we will all have a good old sing-song.

Now and again I will venture into town, although it is a bit traumatic to be in a big crowd. If Glenda is shopping in a precinct, I might back my chair into a corner where I know that I can't be knocked. Then I can feel more secure and can watch the world without worrying.

Occasionally Glenda will take me into shops to buy me something. If she likes something I will encourage her to buy it, but if she tries to buy something for me I will probably say, 'I don't need a new shirt. I've got plenty of them. Put it back!' It is true that I am tempted to do myself down, to think, 'I'm in a wheelchair. It doesn't matter what I look like.' I could so easily lose my sense of self-worth. But I do want to look good, to have a decent haircut and to dress smartly when we go on special outings together — for Glenda's sake more than anything else.

Sometimes I will try things on — not trousers but cardigans or jackets. I bought some shoes once, but my feet swelled with the arthritis and later I couldn't get them on. I had similar difficulties with a pair of boots. I wore them for a while but they rubbed and gave me two ingrowing toenails. For several days after that I had to go around in socks just so that my feet could get better. I soaked them in salt water and was delighted to see my toenails recover. I didn't fancy having the doctor rip them out — even after all that I had been through! So most of the time I go around in slippers, and when it gets cold, I transfer to a pair of furry boots which are one size too big so that I can get into them.

People react to me in various ways. Christians have never been hostile towards me or treated me as though I were mentally incapable. The majority accept me totally, while the rest react with indifference. I can't reach out to people because I am restricted by my wheelchair, so I have to rely on their responding to me. Sometimes I make eye contact with someone across a room. He might smile warmly or return a stony gaze. If I don't get any positive comeback I don't resent him. I always try to maintain a good heart towards everyone.

But I have had to face some negative reactions outside the church. Occasionally people are indifferent, wary or embarrassed, while others are plain hostile. I can now identify with minority groups who face hatred and prejudice. When I was fit I tended to despise the disabled, so it has been good for me to face up honestly to my own bad attitudes. Fortunately, only a few people are spiteful. They see me and think, 'There's something wrong with that man. I don't want anything to do with him.' Then they pull a grim face and refuse to respond to me.

Most people, however, are very kind and friendly. They realise that the disabled need to be accepted and treated like normal people and often go out of their way to help. They open doors for us and offer to negotiate the chair over a step. Society is far more disability-aware than ever before, and sometimes total strangers will stop and engage me in conversation.

Some people feel awkward if they remain standing to talk to me, but I find it quite natural. I don't mind if people kneel in front of me, but I really don't like it when they bend over me with their faces about ten centimetres from mine. Then I feel that my space is being invaded and I want to pull away.

On occasions I refuse offers of assistance. I feel almost embarrassed to do that, but I know that people can't help me even when they insist that they can. 'Let me help you put your coat on,' they say. And I reply, 'No thanks. Glenda will do that,' because she knows that she has to pull it off my right shoulder and under my left elbow. Sometimes I have accepted kind offers like this, but the outcome has been far from satisfactory. It is easier just to refuse.

People who know nothing about wheelchairs are often very keen to help with them. 'I'll take you for a walk,' says someone. Now that is good news for a disabled individual who is not in constant pain, but for me it is a terrifying thought. I know what the pavements outside are like. I know that there is no suspension in the chair. I know that every slightly-raised paving stone is going to jar my fragile body. From my point of view, going for a walk is a major undertaking.

Ascending or descending steps is also something of an ordeal for an inexperienced person. Glenda knows how to tackle steps, others have assumed such knowledge and have almost tipped me out of my chair. I warn them what might happen, but many of them think that when I say, 'Be careful ... do this ... don't do that,' I am just being overcautious. That is not so. I just know from experience what works and what doesn't.

Glenda and I have developed a routine. Others often mean well but can actually make things worse. They fail to listen to what I am saying and assume that they know what I need — which is not always the case. It comes through to me as insensitivity. I try to maintain a good attitude towards them and respond in a loving way. But sometimes I wish that they would find out what would really help and not pursue what *they* think would be a good idea.

I encounter a certain amount of insensitivity from other directions too. One day I asked a woman the time and she answered Glenda. And on another occasion we were out in a restaurant. I was ordering the food and every time I said something, the waiter double-checked with Glenda that it was OK before he wrote it down. In the end I leaned over the table and said to her, 'Does he speak English?' I suppose he thought that she was in charge of me. He clearly couldn't cope with the idea that I could initiate anything. When he had trotted off with our order I said to Glenda, 'You wait until he brings the bill. I'll be completely doo-lally then!'

15

Frustrations, Phobias and Fears

If you ask me what I find hardest to cope with, the answer must be 'frustration'. I've got three super kids, all of them Christians, and I long to do things that normal Dads do with their children: take them bowling, swimming—even hug them. I would love to play football or cricket with my son, even walk down the road with him, but even the simplest activities are impossible. They all think of me as an ordinary father but I know that they have found it difficult to adjust to the limitations of my illness.

I would love to be able to do things for Glenda too. I wish I could give her breakfast in bed, collect the children from school, offer to do the shopping when she is busy. But she is always first up and last to bed, on call night and day. And that can be very tiring. I have to be sensitive to her then, because I have often tried to make unrealistic demands on her when she simply can't fulfil them. That is one of the dangers of being in a wheelchair: you forget what it is like to be normal and think that people can do far more than they actually can. Then you become frustrated when they don't respond to your requests.

So one Sunday we might be late leaving for church. I sit there waiting for Glenda, getting more and more anxious about the time. I know that she has got to put my coat on, get me into the car, belt me in, get me out of the car the other end, take me to the lift ... The minutes tick by and I am panicking, pushing Glenda, almost commanding her, 'We're late. Come on. Let's go.' But sometimes she simply doesn't have the physical resources to move any faster.

One evening we might return home at 10.00 or 11.00. She is exhausted but she still has to get me undressed and into bed, so she has to push herself to keep going. When I get tired I tend to talk too much. My body may be restricted, but my mind is racing over things that need to be done. 'Close the curtains,' I will say. 'Put those tapes away. Fetch my Bible. What's that doing there?' I speak out what I want to do myself, but that is hard for Glenda. She hears me issuing her with instructions and has to remind me that she simply can't do six things at once.

I have to recognise that sometimes Glenda is just too busy to help me. Maybe I want to go to the loo and she is trying to cook the dinner and get the children off to their youth groups. She helps me into the lift, the phone rings and while she is answering it, I have to wait. It is frustrating sitting in the lift, particularly if I'm desperate for the toilet, but I know that it is no good yelling at her to come and help me. I would have done that once, but now I just wait patiently for her.

It is frustrating trying to tell Glenda what to do when I am in pain. On one occasion when my knees were bad, she was trying to get me into bed and I was literally screaming with agony. I knew that she didn't want to hurt me but she couldn't understand what I was asking her to do.

The frustrations are there, but we are not dominated by them. We have learnt the secret of being content in our circumstances. When we are battling through busy and testing times, we pray and God gives us a tremendous sense of peace in our hearts.

I have struggled with agoraphobia too — not so much the fear of going out as a problem with large spaces around me. I first noticed it when I was still able to walk, just before I had to start using the wheelchair. At that time the disease was steadily tilting me forward and making me think that I was going to lose my balance and fall over.

One evening we went to the Albert Hall to hear Handel's *Messiah*. They put us in the top gallery. I walked up there OK but when I looked over the balcony I started to panic and cling to Glenda. I felt as if I were going to fall. I tried to fight it but couldn't. In the end, I turned to Glenda and said, 'I can't stay here. I've got to go down.' They found us seats on a lower level and after that I was fine.

The agoraphobia reared its head again when I was at Downs Bible Week in Plumpton. One night I was asked to sit with some leaders on the platform. I accepted the invitation even though I knew that the experience was going to be hard for me. 'I've got to beat it,' I thought and went up. But when I looked down into the space in front of me I was seized with terror, started to breathe heavily and thought that I was going to pass out. 'Lord, help me,' I prayed. Right through the message I sat and battled to overcome it.

The same thing happened at another Downs, but this time I was determined to conquer my fear. 'With my God I can leap over a wall,' I said to myself and I prayed and trusted God. As a wave of panic swept over me I relaxed and said, 'Lord, you can help me.' The feelings of anxiety subsided and I was fine. I have not suffered the same way since then.

But I do continue to have vertigo, sometimes very badly. One day when I sat up in bed the room started going up like a lift and when I lay down it was spinning round and round. Getting dressed was really hard because I kept feeling that Glenda was pulling me over. It is not usually that bad, but the room often spins a little — sometimes when I am just about to preach. Then I have to fight to keep going.

I have also had to beware of a fear of illness. I don't have a lot of resistance to common sicknesses. If I get a cold, it often develops into a chest infection which is serious because I have only a third of normal breathing capacity. At one time I was very prone to infections but more recently I have been able to fight them off. The reason for that is a combination of prayer and practical wisdom. I ask God for protection, eat better and try to keep away from people who are not well. But it is a struggle not to worry about catching something because I know how much it is going to affect me.

I may be in a worship meeting when someone immediately behind me starts to cough and snuffle. Instead of worshipping God, I am thinking, 'He's got a cold. Why didn't he stay at home?' Then if I do catch something, I am tempted to resent him and complain to Glenda, 'If he'd sat somewhere else, I wouldn't have got this.' Then the love of Jesus goes out of the window. But it probably wasn't his fault at all. In all likelihood, I got the bug off someone else. So I battle between fear and faith. Half of me says, 'I'm going to get this infection and it could put me in bed for weeks,' while the other half declares, 'God can protect you. Trust Him.' It is a constant battle not to allow fear to dominate.

The same concerns surface in the physical realm. My body is terribly fragile and sometimes people don't realise that. They accidentally knock the wheelchair or brush past my knees and it really hurts me. So in worship meetings both Glenda and I are watching to see if anyone is likely to bash into me. Children make me particularly anxious. One day a little boy came up to me with a wooden toy in his hand. 'Hello,' I said. He just looked at me and then hit me hard on the knee with his toy. I felt like screaming.

I am not fearful that something might happen to Glenda, but naturally I would be put into a predicament if she were taken ill for any length of time. She understands my fragility and knows what to do. I depend so much on her. When I was in hospital the nurses were often unsure about how to look after me so they asked her to help them. I constantly pray that God will protect and watch over her. He has done that and I thank Him for His grace in keeping her strong. It is part of His provision for me.

The difficulties come. I have had to learn not to fear them but to press through and overcome. Constantly I look to God for the inner strength to face the demands of each day, and He helps me.

Someone once asked me, 'Do you cry together?'

I recalled one occasion when we were camping at Downs. We felt so blessed to be there but it was cold and I was in so much pain. One night we just wept together.

Glenda has spent a lot of time crying when we've tried to get me washed in the shower. She feels for me because I am in pain. I tell her, 'It's OK, don't cry. I'll be all right soon.' Sometimes we take so long that the hot water runs out. Then the drain gets blocked, so she's trying to sort that out. I'm saying, 'I'm getting cold.' She's saying, 'I know, I'll help you in a minute.' She is in the middle of washing my hair and is boiling hot. Finally she gets me out of the bathroom and by comparison, the bedroom feels like a fridge to me. She tries to dress me, cope with my terrible pain — and the tears flow.

She will occasionally go off and cry on her own — when she really doesn't understand why these things are happening to us. Then she pours it all out to God. When you think about it, that is the best time to cry. The Bible says that God notices our tears and puts them in a bottle. I am not a very tearful person, but I have sometimes wept when I am thinking about life and other people. I will cry for Glenda and the children. I will think, 'Lord, I wish I could do things with them,' and I picture myself running, laughing, enjoying their company. But God is good and His love fills my heart with joy and hope. As a family we enjoy His presence and provision. One day I will walk and run again. But right now I can rejoice in my sufferings because I believe that He is producing good things in me.

16
Ministry Trip

It's 6.15 in the morning. The alarm rings. Glenda gets up and brings me a cup of tea which, as usual, I drink through a straw. At 7.00 I need to get out of bed. My legs feel numb and my circulation seems to have stopped. I can barely move my feet. As Glenda lifts the duvet over my bent knees it causes one of them to go into a spasm. I can't stop it shaking and the pain makes me catch my breath. Glenda helps me to get dressed. She does everything slowly and gently but the pain is still excruciating. At 7.30 I have a quick wash—having shaved the previous night to save time. I get into the lift and go downstairs. After a quick cup of tea and a biscuit, Glenda helps me put on my jacket and slippers and loads me into the car.

I'm due to preach in Winchester so we make our way for the M3. I'm cold and can hardly wait for the heater to warm up. Glenda turns the corner. My legs swing from side to side which causes pain. We arrive twenty minutes before the morning meeting begins. Greg Haslam greets me warmly as the new church building fills with about four hundred people. I enjoy the lively, uplifting worship, then I prepare to speak. I forget about my aches and pains as I share what God has given me to say. It's such a privilege to be His spokesman. After the meeting people speak to me at the door and we go back to Greg and Ruth Haslam's house for lunch and a time of excellent fellowship.

At 3.15 we are on the road again — this time to Bournemouth where I'm due to speak at Lansdowne Baptist Church. The pastor, Steve Brady, was at London Bible College with me. We try to follow the directions but get lost several times and arrive at Steve's house at 5.00. Brenda, Steve's wife, has multiple sclerosis and is resting when we get there. My heart is touched as I watch Steve serving her and the family. We crack jokes, have some tea and then make our way to the church.

I'm wheeled round the side and into the vestry. Several deacons greet me, then I'm pushed through the door that leads into the main building. Six hundred people have packed the church. I gaze around at the faces and feel the same sense of expectation that I got when I preached to a few thousand at Stoneleigh Bible Week in 1991.

We worship together. It's tremendous. Someone plays the guitar and sings. Someone else gives a testimony and then Steve interviews me before I preach.

'Tell us about some of your background. Where did you live when you were a child?'
'In Leytonstone, then we moved to Suffolk.'

'You went to London Bible College, didn't you? Were you a Christian?'
'I think so! — Yes, of course I was.

'From there you went to be a pastor in South Harrow, didn't you?'
'That's right. I went to Roxeth Green Free Church. It was on a vast estate so we had a ready-made mission field. Then I planted a new church in Stanmore, Middlesex.'

'Haven't you planted another church since?'
'Yes. In South Oxhey. The church there has grown tremendously. In fact, the mother church is now back to its original size.'

'You're in a wheelchair now. What's the *prognosis* and *diagnosis*?'
'Can I have an interpretation, please?'
(The congregation laughs.)

'It sounded good to me when I said it,' Steve replies. 'I didn't understand it myself.' (There's more laughter.)
'Don't you speak to me in Italian, Mr Brady,' I cry. (This makes him laugh.)

I explain about my arthritic disease and then after a hymn, I begin to preach on rejoicing in suffering from Romans 5. It's a message which features an imaginary phonecall with the apostle Paul and is generally received very well. I pick up a telephone receiver and chat to Paul and to the congregation.

Hello, Paul! Wonderful to hear you! How are you? **You're rejoicing!** Oh good! You've been preaching the gospel everywhere? Great! How did things go at Philippi? You had a few problems? What sort of problems? You were put in prison! Paul, that's terrible. What happened? You healed a slave girl ... they flogged you ... put you in the stocks ... and you were stinging? Oh — you were singing! I bet that brought the house down! You and Silas were **rejoicing** because you were suffering for Jesus. Paul, you're amazing!

What's that? You've been doing some open airs. But you had some problems with them as well? So have we. Last week our

P.A. broke down! You were stoned! Paul, that's terrible! You must have been very upset. What happened? You were preaching the gospel, the crowd turned nasty and started throwing stones? Paul, that's really awful. How do you feel? **You're rejoicing!** You're going to do some more open airs? Paul, is that wise? You seem to be having such a bad time! Do try and look after yourself!

Shipwreck? What shipwreck? Paul, I didn't know you were involved in a shipwreck! That's your third shipwreck! Paul, do you have to travel by boat? You must be devastated? You're not devastated. **You're rejoicing!**

Paul, have you shared this with the brothers? What about Demas? What do you mean, he's left you? What about the other brothers? They've left you too! Paul, that's the worst thing that could possibly happen!

I know, we should rejoice in the Lord always. No, you don't have to say it again, Paul! How can you rejoice at a time like this? I know Habakkuk did — but he was only short of figs and milk!

You've been flogged, put in prison, stoned, shipwrecked three times and now all the brothers have left you. Things couldn't get any worse, could they?

Thorn? What thorn? Paul, have you been

> gardening again? I told you to stick to tent making! Oh, it's not that kind of thorn. It's a problem. What sort of problem? A big problem! You can tell me what it is. No ... really? That's terrible. Oh Paul! How do you feel about this terrible problem? **You're rejoicing!** His grace is sufficient for you? Paul, you're incredible. God bless. Yes, I'll keep rejoicing! Bye.

The response is tremendous. Frequently the message is interrupted by peals of laughter. I look round and think, 'They're thoroughly enjoying this and I'm having a great time too.' But, most important of all, I know that the Word is taking root in their hearts.

My message is recorded on audio cassette and on video. After the meeting, several of them buy my 'How to ...' book, *Facing Life's Problems*. I sign copies for them. Disabled people talk to me and I encourage them to prove God's grace and press through their difficulties.

Glenda and I follow Steve to the house where we are staying for the night. It's a beautiful place and supper is waiting for us. By 11.00 I'm quite exhausted. I'm carried upstairs. The bed is too low so we have to put it on blocks. Glenda gets me undressed. I have to take two painkillers because my knees are so bad. The pain subsides and I start to fall asleep. It's a wonderful feeling.

Finally Glenda gets herself ready for bed. It has been a long day for us both, but God has been glorified and like Paul, we're rejoicing.

17
Great Expectation

It started in the mid 1980s. One of the women in the church came up to me before a morning worship meeting and said, 'I dreamt about you last night. You were walking into a room and you were straight.' I thanked her but really didn't think that the dream had much significance at that time.

The following week we were having a break with the family in Fordham. While we were there, we visited a couple called Ken and Pat in Isleham. Immediately she saw me, Pat said, 'Frank, I dreamt about you this week.' Then she told me that she had seen me walking into a room and I was straight. I was amazed.

When we returned home someone else phoned me. 'I've had a dream about you,' she said. 'Don't tell me,' I replied. 'You saw me walk into a room and I was straight.' 'How did you know?' she asked in astonishment, and I explained.

Since those first three dreams there have been

over two dozen others. Each one is the same and each comes from an independent source. The people who relate them to me think that the dream is rather insignificant, but I am thrilled every time. It seems to me that every few months God is keen to remind me that one day I am going to be healed.

Naturally I have shared my conviction with the church and with the leaders of the New Frontiers churches with which we are associated. They have been very supportive and have taken some of the loneliness away from my situation. They love me, stand with me in the pain and pray specifically both for my healing and for God's grace to be with me in my suffering. A group of people in the Harrow church pray for me every day, and on occasions the elders have prayed publicly and anointed me with oil.

The prayers for my complete healing have not yet been answered, but prayer has certainly played a large part in seeing me through things like chest infections and other minor ailments. On one occasion my skin was flaking quite badly, but several people prayed that God would put the oil back in it and He did. The next day my skin was smooth. He has healed a very dry patch on my hip and various pains in my hands and ankles. All these answers are encouragements to me. Whenever Christians pray for me I feel loved, strengthened and comforted. Glenda appreciates it when people reach out to her too.

When you believe that God is going to do something, you hang onto it in faith — even when your conviction flies in the face of reason. Humanly speaking, I am an impossible case. When my consultant wrote to my doctor to give him some details about me, he said that I was in a serious condition and added, 'Unless God "supervenes", which is Mr Gamble's conviction, there is no hope.' But with God, all things are possible and all the medical people who have treated me have discovered that I am believing Him for healing. Even my children are telling their school friends to expect a miracle.

A number of people have tried to explain why I have not been healed. 'Your problem is caused by sin,' say some, while others favour the need for emotional release or deliverance from demons. Although it is true that sickness is ultimately the result of Satan's work, it is not right to say that believers should never be ill. Job's three comforters attempted to give him sound advice on why he was suffering. Their arguments might have been very appropriate for a sinful person, but in Job's case, the friends were barking up the wrong tree.

I have often sought God about barriers to my healing. I have asked Him if I need to repent, consulted Him about my background and considered demonic roots. I want to be open to

Him and if He tells me that there is something that needs to be sorted out, I will respond immediately. In fact, I would do as He said even if I didn't have my illness. I am not obeying Him because I want to be healed but because I love Him. The disease is His will for me now and it will bring Him glory.

Some people have attempted to force healing on me. That can be quite frightening because I think that I am going to be hurt. On one occasion Glenda and I had just arrived at a social event in someone's garden when a woman rushed up to us and immediately started crying out to God for my healing. 'Stand up in the name of Jesus!' she shouted and tried to yank me up by my arm. Glenda, who was gripping my other arm, was battling to hold me down while I was pleading with her not to let go. Eventually the hostess yelled across the garden at the woman, who released her grip and went away. She avoided us for the rest of the evening.

That is an extreme example of what has happened to me. Sometimes the approach is not as dramatic, but the motivation still seems wrong. While I have been in a wheelchair I have noticed that my senses have become very acute, particularly my hearing. I am also very conscious of individuals and their reactions to me. Sometimes people come up to me and say, 'Can I pray with you?' and I reply, 'No, I'd rather you didn't. But please pray privately.' I sense that their motivation is misplaced. They are viewing me as a prize picking — if they can get me healed, wow! So for that reason they make a beeline for me.

Certainly God can perform His wonders through total strangers, but they must have the right motivation. Many people have asked if they can pray with me and I have been very happy to let them do so. Why? Because I know that they understand my situation, that they love me and have been praying regularly for me. When they pray I sense their warmth. Their prayers bless and comfort me and I feel sure that God has sent them.

Naturally I have had to face disappointment. On several occasions I thought that God would heal me and my hopes were dashed. I really believed that I would walk out of one particular conference. In fact, before we left home, Glenda put one of my belts in her handbag because she knew that if I stood up my trousers would fall down! But there was no healing.

Now and again I am tempted to feel sorry for myself, but I have always resisted it because self-pity is a never-ending downward spiral. It leads to resentment towards God and other people, then it turns to anger and finally despair — because you think that there is no answer to your problem. So if someone says to me, or even to Glenda, 'It must be really hard for you,' we will be honest but refuse to allow ourselves to be drawn into self-pity. We know that it is not the right road.

Anger at God is not helpful either. You cry out against Him if you lose your consciousness of His love, goodness and purpose for your life. Only once or twice have I succumbed to the temptation to get angry with the Lord. At the time when I was transferring to the wheelchair, when I was becoming more disabled, I protested to Him, 'Can't you see what this is doing to Glenda? Don't you understand? Why don't you do something when you can see how bad it is?' Through that experience God revealed things in me that I thought were not there. He dealt with me and reminded me that He did know what it was like and that He did care. His timing is perfect and He will heal me only when He is ready.

Both Glenda and I rejoice when God heals other people. There is no sense of envy in our hearts. We once heard a tape by Jennifer Rees-Larcombe and wept when she shared the difficulties that she encountered through being in a wheelchair. We identified so closely with her. Then when she talked about her healing, we cried for joy.

I try to be sympathetic towards others who are in pain. Sometimes their aches might be very small by comparison with mine, but I won't despise them and think, ‘Oh, he’s only got a touch of backache’ or ‘She’s merely got a cold.’ If they are hurting I feel with them. Of course, if I sense that someone is drifting into self-pity, I will probably think, ‘He’s giving up too easily. If I let him get away with that, he’ll start falling back from things that he should be doing.’ Then I will encourage him to draw on God’s grace and push through.

I am grateful to the many people who have not given up on me — even in the face of apparent failure. The widow had to battle hard before the unjust judge granted her justice. And Elijah, a man like us, was not immediately given an answer to his prayer. Seven times he prayed earnestly and looked for the rain. Then the cloud appeared and it came. Jesus wants us not to lose heart but to persist in prayer until the ‘rain’ comes — even when we can’t see it approaching. The results of prayer may not yet be evident in my situation, but the prayers themselves have not been lost. I sense that when people pray for me they effectively put another speck of sand on the scales, and one day God will break in and heal me.

No one has ever told me how God will do that, but I don’t think that it will be a gradual thing. If it were, I would probably have to go through a reverse process of pain and readjustment, and I think that is unlikely. So I have tended to believe that the miracle will be sudden, that God will loosen my joints and make me completely whole. I might have a measure of weakness until the muscles have grown strong, but not necessarily. The man who was crippled from birth suddenly started walking, leaping and praising God, so his muscles must have been restored immediately, as was his ability to walk.

A lot of things will arise from my healing — not least of all, the strengthening of faith. Many Christians who have been praying for me will be thrilled. But I'll try to be disciplined and resist the temptation to accept every invitation to speak and share my testimony. Initially I'll spend some quality time with my wife and family. Both Glenda and I will need to make huge adjustments, and I'll simply want to enjoy her company and give something back to her for all that she has given to me.

Miracles don't always result in ongoing zeal and vibrant faith. They can lead to apathy. After a while Lazarus, and everyone who heard about his experience, would have settled down to normal life. Some people who believed in Jesus then may even have backslidden later. The same is true today. God can do something incredible in your life but you still drift from Him. When God heals me I don't want the miracle to go to my head or get me sidetracked from His plan for my life. I am keen to maintain my zeal, to bear fruit for Him and to continue building the church.

Meanwhile, I'm going through a process of refinement so that when the time comes, I'm ready.

18
Shadow of Death

When you are praying for one thing it is hard when the opposite thing seems to be happening. I didn't think that my condition could get much worse than it was, but I was wrong.

In October 1990 I was feeling breathless and very weak, so I went to the doctor who gave me antibiotics and booked me in for a routine chest X-ray. Glenda had to drag me out of bed to get to that appointment because I was feeling so unwell. When the hospital doctor had looked at the results, she informed me that my left lung had collapsed and I would need to have a pipe inserted into my side to take away the air that was trapped between my lung and its lining , which is called the pleura. A nurse immediately wheeled me down the corridor towards accident and emergency.

On the way we passed a room where some doctors were examining my X-ray. 'Come and look at this,' said one of them. 'I've never seen anyone with a pneumo-thorax as bad as that.'

When we arrived I was suddenly surrounded by doctors and nurses and there were syringes all over the place. I had always been a bit squeamish about hospitals and needles but strangely, on this occasion, I was not anxious at all. I felt calm and secure, as if everything were in God's hands. After the tests I was taken to an operating theatre where my side was cut open and a pipe inserted into my lung. I had only a local anaesthetic so I was conscious the whole time.

I chatted to the doctor as she worked on me. When the drain was in place she left the room and I suddenly went into an uncontrollable coughing fit. The pipe in my lung had triggered off a reaction and I started to panic because I couldn't breathe. Fortunately, I soon stopped coughing and was taken up to the ward. Not realising how fragile I was, an orderly roughly took hold of my legs to transfer me onto the bed. I let out a cry of pain. That moment was worse than the whole operation that I had just been through.

As I lay on the bed the man in the bed next to me asked if I was all right. 'I'm fine,' I said. 'I'm rejoicing!' 'How can you rejoice at a time like this?' he questioned. 'Because I know that God is working for my good,' I answered. 'Are you a Christian?' he asked. 'Yes I am,' I replied. 'So am

I,' he declared joyfully. I was amazed that God had provided a Christian right next to me.

I was in hospital for a fortnight. During that time I often wondered what God was doing in my life. Within two weeks of my going home I was back in hospital because my lung collapsed again. I was with the family for Christmas but felt incredibly weak. Poor Glenda didn't have only one invalid on her hands, but two. A couple of days before Christmas, our son Adam had fallen off his skateboard and broken his leg.

In January 1991 my lung collapsed for the third time. The doctor tried to draw the air off by putting a needle into my back, but that didn't work so some antibiotic dust was put into my lung to try and make it stick. Even though I had a painkilling injection it was the most excruciating experience that I have ever had. I came out of hospital and was back again within 48 hours when my lung collapsed for the fourth time. They put another drain into my side and I stayed for a further week.

At this point I seriously began to wonder what was going to happen to me and talked to Glenda about the possibility of my dying. Death frightened me — even though I knew the scriptural teaching about it being gain for God's children. I worked through my fear by thinking over what the Bible said about death and reminding myself that whether I lived or died, I belonged to the Lord. In case anything happened to me, I decided to write a goodbye letter to Glenda. I hid it among my belongings.

I thought a great deal about the dreams and prophecies that people had shared with me over the years. They all indicated that God would heal me. One day I read in the Psalms, 'Your promise preserves my life.' 'God will heal me sometime in the future,' I thought. 'But for now He promises that I won't die but see His goodness in the land of the living.'

Mr Townsend, a specialist from Harefield Hospital, was consulted about the ongoing problem with my lung. On the morning that I was due to see him, two obscure verses in Job seemed to leap out of the Bible at me. 'Each is so close to the next that no air can pass between them. They are joined fast to one another, they cling together and cannot be parted.' I had already prayed that God would heal my lung, but that day I sensed a new rise of faith in my heart.

When Mr Townsend saw me he suggested that I go to Harefield and have a general anaesthetic so that angel dust could be sprayed into my lung to cause scarring of the pleura. This would do what the antibiotic dust had failed to do, namely make the lung stick to its lining. 'We want to join the lung and the pleura fast together so that no air can pass between them,' he said. I was amazed at his words because the verses in Job were saying exactly the same thing.

That weekend I was admitted to Harefield Hospital. I knew that a general anaesthetic presented a real threat to me because of my physical weakness and severe disability. But I no longer feared death and I felt very peaceful and secure in God. The night before my operation the anaesthetist came to see me. He took one look at me and put his head in his hands. 'This is a disaster,' he said. 'We won't be able to ventilate you during the operation.' 'What about a tracheotomy?' I asked. 'It may come to that,' he replied. 'Well, why not give me a shot of morphine and do it while I'm awake?' I continued. 'That's another possibility,' he answered, and shaking his head, he went off. I turned over and went to sleep. I was not worried or fearful. The Lord was my keeper.

The following morning I took a tablet for the pre-med and I was wheeled into the theatre. I told the nurses and doctors that I was a Christian and said that if anything happened to me I would be safe in heaven. I fell asleep somewhere between John 3:16 and Romans 8:28! They were probably very relieved! Some hours later I woke up to find a drip in my arm and a pipe in my lung which was connected to a suction machine. Within a short time I was eating and feeling much stronger.

A couple of days later Mr Townsend came round to see me. He told me that things had gone well but that he had only managed to put a minimal amount of angel dust into my lung. 'It seemed to be pretty well stuck,' he told me. I felt an immediate concern about the word 'minimal' because I wanted him to tell me that he had put loads of angel dust into me and that I was well and truly stuck up! That afternoon they removed the drain and X-rayed me to see if the lung was still OK. Everything was fine. I went home that evening.

I felt weak, but happy to be with my family and happier still to be alive. The following day I was lying in bed wondering if the small amount of angel dust would be sufficient to stick my lung when I sensed that God was speaking to me. 'Do you remember the verses in Job that I gave you?' He said. Then He added, 'Frank, I stuck your lung.' I replied, 'Lord, how do I know this is you speaking to me?'

He answered, 'This will be a sign for you. Tell Glenda to get your *Read the Bible in One Year* book and find the New Testament reading for today. In it you will find these words, "They are no longer two but one," and "What God has joined let not man separate." '

I called Glenda and asked her to get the book but I didn't tell her why. I had not looked at it for over a month so I didn't have a clue what the reading for that day would be. Glenda started to read the New Testament passage to me. It didn't seem likely that the words would show up. Then there they were, in the very last paragraph, 'They are no longer two but one' and 'What God has joined let not man separate.' God had healed my lung. No wonder Mr Townsend could get only a minimal amount of angel dust into my lung. Didn't he say it was already stuck up? I shared with Glenda what God had said and we rejoiced together.

Later God spoke to me again. One day while I was worshipping Him I saw a vision of two hands wringing out a wet cloth. When it was wrung out, it dropped open and on it was written the word *devoted*. The hands then began to wring out the cloth a second time. It fell open and on it was written the word *wholehearted*. The hands wrung out the cloth again and this time I read the word *loving*. Finally, the hands wrung out the cloth so that there wasn't a drop of moisture left in it. It fell open and on it were the words *faithful unto death*. At this point the Lord spoke to me. 'Frank,' He said. 'I've been wringing you out so that everything in your life that displeases me will go. When my work in you is complete, you will be all of those four things that you saw written on the cloth.'

19
On Fire for Him

When you have faced death, you suddenly have a new perspective on life. 'Am I ready to die?' you think, and God challenges you to question whether you are living for the present day or pursuing something eternal. The Bible says that this world will one day come to an end so it makes a lot of sense to seek God's Kingdom now rather than wait until it is too late.

I sought God more earnestly when my lung was collapsing. I recognised afresh that I belonged to Him and told Him that He could use me in any way He liked. I also asked Him to bless whatever I did. Since that day I have been increasingly aware of His presence with me and of a widening ministry.

For a while now I have been responsible for the oversight of five churches in my region. I bring direction to the leaders and the local churches that they serve. Until recently, this responsibility was coupled with my work as lead elder of the Harrow church, not to mention an ever-growing preaching and teaching ministry. I have also been involved in writing magazine articles and, more recently, books — my workbook on suffering came out in 1991. Needless to say, as I received more and more invitations to speak, I began to feel a certain amount of tension between this ministry and my leadership of the local church.

Then one day Terry Virgo encouraged me to step into a more public ministry which could still be based in Harrow. The following week I received a number of invitations to speak which confirmed to me that God was guiding me in this direction. Terry, the elders and I agreed that such a ministry would make it difficult for me to remain lead elder of the Harrow church, so I handed the reins over to Ken Shelley, a godly man who had worked alongside me for a number of years. A great sense of relief swept over me as I pulled out of lead eldership. For the previous few months I had not been able to lead effectively and sensed that the church was beginning to suffer because of this. I also felt greater freedom to accept speaking invitations that I might otherwise have turned down.

I am amazed that God has given me this new ministry. I am physically weak, and don't think of myself as special at all. But He has chosen something that is weak and foolish to confound the strong and wise. Since I have been in a wheelchair, my ministry has expanded considerably, and people have been encouraged through my testimony and my preaching of the Word. God's grace is sufficient for me and His power is made perfect in my weakness (2 Cor. 12:9). When I was at Bible college we used to say, 'Any old bush will do.' We were referring to the burning bush which caught Moses' attention. The bush was just an ordinary bush. The difference was that it had the fire of God in it. God uses weak and foolish people. The important thing is that they are full of His Spirit and Word — on fire for Him.

God has given me a message to proclaim. Above all, it is a message of encouragement for individuals who doubt the love and goodness of God. Some of them say, 'God can't be very loving if He's letting me go through this,' while others think, 'He doesn't understand' or 'He doesn't care' or 'He's punishing me.' If you don't know God's character, you are liable to look at your problems in this way.

A compass needle will always point to the north. It won't lie to you but will faithfully tell you where you are. Sometimes you have to trust it because if you don't, you might think that north is somewhere else. The Bible is our reference point, true down to the last detail. You read it and it tells you where you are. Sometimes you just have to trust it, otherwise you might think that God's character is something other than what it is.

So what does the Bible say about God and suffering? It says that God is love and that He is infinitely compassionate and merciful towards us. It tells us that He demonstrated His love for us by sending His Son to die in agony on a cross to take the punishment for our sins. Love cannot pay a higher price. Since Jesus Himself suffered, He is able to help us in our suffering because He understands exactly how we feel when we go through pain and difficulties. If we believe that He is good, it will affect the way in which we look at every situation that we face.

The Bible teaches that this world is under Satan's influence and that he is ultimately responsible for all sickness and pain. If we think of creation as a great computer, then Satan is an evil hacker who is intent on spoiling everything that God has made. By disarming Satan at the cross, Jesus has done something about pain and suffering — He has dealt with the root of the problem. So it's not that He doesn't care. If He treated us as we deserved, we would all be condemned to eternal agony in hell. But God is so gracious that He sent Jesus to suffer for us, so that one day we would be totally free from pain with Him in heaven.

God is allowing me to suffer. I don't fully

understand all the reasons, but I trust Him completely because I know what He is like. When I look at my suffering in the light of eternity, I realise that my present troubles are slight momentary afflictions. What is suffering for a short time now compared with eternal glory to come? I would rather be in this wheelchair and know that I am going to heaven than be fully fit and on my way to hell. For unbelievers, suffering is meaningless and leads to despair. But for Christians, it produces perseverance, godly character and hope (Rom. 5:3,4). That is why we are exhorted to rejoice in suffering. God is doing something worthwhile in our lives.

Some people look at me and say, 'Surely you battle over your situation. You must feel some resentment towards God, have some doubts about His goodness, experience some sense of self-pity.' I say, 'No,' to each of these things. I can honestly say that I have no ongoing internal struggles. I am totally confident that God is good, that His ways are completely just and that He is fulfilling His perfect plan for my life. I don't look at God in the light of my problems but at my problems in the light of God.

Even after I have said these things, a number of people still find it hard to believe how secure I am in God. But I can say only what I know to be the truth. I do not say one thing in public and then act out a different story in private. 'So what's the secret?' they ask. 'How do you manage to cope?' And I reply, 'God enables me to triumph. What you see is His grace working in my life and His peace in my heart'.

Psalm 62:8 has always meant a great deal to me. It says, 'Trust in him at all times, O people; pour out your hearts to him, for God is our refuge.' Whenever I feel weary or discouraged I pour out my heart to Him and He never fails me. I know that 'in all things God works for the good of those who love him, who have been called according to his purpose' (Rom. 8:28).

It is by the grace of God that I am what I am — hard pressed sometimes, but not crushed; perplexed, but not in despair; struck down, but not destroyed; at times sorrowful, but always rejoicing. I always carry around in my body the death of Jesus, so that the life of Jesus may also be revealed in my body. His joy is my strength, and through Him I can do all things. If Paul could conquer, so can I. If I can conquer, then so can you.

If this book encourages you to look to God for strength and help to overcome your problems and suffering, then it will have achieved the purpose for which it was written. You may be ill or facing huge difficulties. Perhaps you have discounted yourself and assumed that God can't use you because of your circumstances. Well, don't give up on God because He has not given up on you. He has a plan for you and wants your life to shine in spite of your troubles and pain. By grace, Paul mastered his 'thorn in the flesh' and worked hard; by grace you too can triumph over your difficulties and live for the glory of Jesus.

At the close of this book it would have been wonderful to be able to say, 'The Lord has healed me.' He has not. But I am not giving up hope of that momentous event. It is rather like waiting for the Lord's return. I constantly live with the conviction that one day healing will come — God will work the miracle and I will stand up and be totally restored.

But that is not my chief goal. My preoccupation is not so much, 'When am I going to be healed?' as, 'Am I living for the glory of God?' I don't just plan to sit around twiddling my thumbs while God refines me. There is Kingdom work to be done and God wants to be glorified in my weakness as I do it. The glory of His name — that is my focus , whether I am in this wheelchair for another ten or twenty years, or whether I am fully restored tomorrow.

While I wait, life will continue to be hard but God's grace will go on being sufficient. It never runs dry. I constantly rejoice in His love and goodness, knowing without a shadow of a doubt that He will complete the work that He has begun in me.